Playwrights Teach Playwriting 2

A Guide to Writing Plays and Teaching Playwriting

by America's Master Playwrights

Other titles by Joan Herrington

Playwrights Teach Playwriting (Smith and Kraus)
The Playwrights Muse (Routledge)
I Ain't Sorry for Nothin' I Done: August Wilson's Process of Play-writing (Limelight)
August Wilson in an Hour (Smith and Kraus)

PLAYWRIGHTS TEACH PLAYWRITING 2

A GUIDE TO WRITING PLAYS AND TEACHING PLAYWRITING

BY AMERICA'S MASTER PLAYWRIGHTS

Joan Herrington

With Crystal Brian

A SMITH AND KRAUS BOOK   2018

A Smith and Kraus Book
177 Lyme Road, Hanover, NH 03755
editorial 603.643.6431 To Order 1.877.668.8680
www.smithandkraus.com

Playwrights Teach Playwriting 2
A Guide to Writing Plays and Teaching Playwriting
by America's Master Playwrights
Copyright © 2017 by Joan Herrington
All rights reserved.

Manufactured in the United States of America

ISBN: 9781575259192
Library of Congress Control Number: 2017958539

Typesetting and layout by Elizabeth E. Monteleone
Cover by Emily Herrington
Cover photographs:
  Jon Robin Baitz by Daniel Gonzalez
  Steven Dietz by Bret Brookshire
  Beth Henley by Michael Childers
  Lucas Hnath by Rebecca Martinez
  Quiara Alegria Hudes by Emma Pratte
  Lisa Krone by Eva Weiss
  Carlos Murillo by Andrea Tichy
  Suzan-Lori Parks by Tammy Shell
  Sarah Ruhl Courtesy the John D. and Catherine T. MacArthur Foundation
  Octavio Solis by Anne Hamersky

For information about custom editions, special sales, education and corporate purchases, please contact Smith and Kraus at editor@smithandkraus.com or 603.643.6431

Joan Herrington thanks her daughters Emily and Sarah, who inspire her always, and Tucker Rafferty, for his unwavering support. She also thanks Crystal Brian for her invaluable assistance in compiling this volume.

Crystal Brian thanks her daughter, Amy Van Ness; Horton Foote; Tina Howe for inspiration; and Andy Corwin, Kevin Daly, and David Ives for their encouragement.

The editors wish to acknowledge the inspiration of Paula Vogel in the process of creating this book and to thank the writers herein for generously sharing their knowledge.

This book would not have been possible without the remarkable work of our editorial assistant, Cara Beth Heath.

CONTENTS

FOREWORD

All of the writers included in this book are important, in our time, to our theater, and to the texture of our lives—especially in these difficult, er, *Times*. What better antidote to so-called *Fake News* is there than the mysterious and prophetic jibber-jabber of our writers for the stage? Consider how weird and wonderful it all is: Someone, a genius and/or a demon perhaps, makes marks on paper, many of them (and all of them incomprehensible to disciples of *Fake News*); these are then shown to other people who then speak and move about accordingly, enacting events both possible and probable; both impossible and improbable; still other people observe these, in real time (whatever that is), and in live space (aha!); and as a result experience powerful emotions and thoughts—some familiar but often as not, many not at all familiar. All this is perfect antidote to all that oppresses us in our public lives.

ITEM

We often talk about "talent" and "creativity" as though these were a universal, a kind of *tofu* of the soul, identical in all respects and in all instances; and certainly so in the better class of our theaters. And certainly the better class of our theater critics tend to discuss all instances of talent, genius even, as though this were the case. But it seems to me what is remarkable about theater writers who have achieved something remarkable in their work, as these all have, is how different they all are, one from the other; and also frequently how different they are, and what their work is, from what they had been up to earlier.

With every instance of a truly remarkable theater, one comes away from the experience almost always surprised. Surprised, shocked, and stunned. Epiphany is at the core of the theater experience.

1

ITEM

Look at the late quartets of Beethoven. They are remarkably different from his earlier work, and often shocked and puzzled his contemporaries. "This is not for you," he once said to an acquaintance who was baffled by his style. "This is for the future," he suggested. Perhaps even Shakespeare did not always know he was *Shakespeare* (even though he had a clue!).

Many of these writers I have known as friends and colleagues; some I have not. But what impresses me so much about their practices as teachers of creative writing for the theater is just how different they are, one from the other, and as an aggregate, how inspiring their differences—their profound uniqueness is! This kind of diversity is as rich as the complex state of the art, and the state of the nation in our time.

—MAC WELLMAN

INTRODUCTION

This book brings together some of the most acclaimed contemporary writers, all of whom have chosen to share their gifts with the next generation of playwrights. It was inspired by Paula Vogel, who saw the need for the ideas and methodologies of our most thoughtful, creative, and innovative writing teachers to be shared. Ten years after publishing *Playwrights Teach Playwriting,* it is time for another volume, capturing a new generation of artists whose classrooms reflect the very best in theory and practice.

The writers included in this book teach an array of students—undergraduates who are writing plays for the first time; undergraduates who have already committed themselves as playwrights; beginning and advanced graduate students; and early career writers. They present an array of approaches to developing and practicing the craft of playwriting, but at the heart of all their work is a profound commitment to developing a unique voice and enabling young writers to discover the form their individual play should take.

Each chapter in this book presents an approach to teaching as different from one another as the plays their authors create. But there are many commonalities in the conversation. First is consideration as to whether playwriting can be taught at all, and if so, how? What can be acquired in the playwriting classroom, and what does the writer need to possess to even begin the difficult task of writing a successful play?

Steven Dietz lists audacity, empathy, guile, and patience as key qualities that any playwright must naturally possess. Jon Robin Baitz writes, "It's hard to be a good playwright if you don't understand the musicality of human speech—if you don't understand that there are rhythms, and that words arranged together in a certain order create a kind of musicality."

3

Lisa Kron adds, "There are aspects of playwriting that can be taught, but can anybody write a play? Probably not. You have to be observant and have a point of view. It helps if you have a sense of humor. You have to be interested in flux more than you're interested in stasis."

Sarah Ruhl believes that "it's crucial for playwrights to have an ear. It's interesting that it goes back to listening, both as a teacher and as a writer. It's very hard to teach having an ear, if you don't have it, if you don't have a sense of the rhythm of language and the rhythm of living speech—it' s almost impossible to teach that."

What, then, can be taught? These writers agree that there are fundamentals and elementary craft elements—structure, plotting, character development—that can be acquired in the playwriting classroom and then clarified through practice. But beyond these basics, where should a teacher focus, or what should a student be able to pursue through a formal study of playwriting? Beth Henley says, "Imagination, observation, and experience (Faulkner's big three) can be encouraged and enhanced."

Jon Robin Baitz believes, "You can teach editing. You can teach them to use as few words a possible or to use as many words as possible depending on the moment." He also says, "The things you can teach are forward movement, the question of how does a plot advance; what's going to happen next is important in a play, no matter how complex or sophisticated it is."

Lucas Hnath notes, "I think building problems and actions into a play—that can be taught. Conflict can be taught."

As quickly as some of these writers identify that which can be taught to advance a writer—and these are only a few from the list—Quiara Hudes makes another key point:

> I don't know that writing can be taught, really, but I know that bad writing habits can be taught. The most important thing is to not have a prescriptive approach to writing. There is not one way to write a play or even three ways to write a play. There are many ways to write plays, so use a diverse set of literature as your starting off point rather than a bulleted list of what ingredients a well-made play must have.

Indeed, ensuring that young writers are not in any way restricted by formal study, many of these playwrights speak to the common idea that there is no formula for writing a play. Ruhl writes, "It's good for writers to realize there's not just one form—the Aristotelian arc."

Several of these writers include exercises where students are challenged to write a "bad play," most often interpreted as one that does not follow conventional rules. The results are sometimes creative launching points for new work. A recurring theme in the words of many of these teachers is the need for writers to truly open themselves to their own work, to listen to their characters, and to allow their imaginations to drive the play.

Octavio Solis wants his students to "simply write without judgment and reasoning—to write from a very different place than they think they are supposed to write." Thus, many of these writers do not necessarily speak to any traditional perspective on "how to write a play."

Lisa Kron feels there are too many rules and bemoans the limitations some forms of study impose on early playwrights.

> I want my students to trust their own imagination, their own impulses and their own voice. How do I say this diplomatically? They have been told there are all these rules for how to write a play and they are trying to figure out how they are going to write a play that would be acceptable. And they ask for a lot of permission. I try to break them of that habit. It's very important to me that my students are open, that they experiment. But this doesn't mean there is not commitment to craft those experiments into a piece of theater that generates that electricity between performer and audience.

Octavio Solis is equally wary:

> The more formal bullet points of playwriting become relevant only when they turn up in the work. Otherwise, when I start talking about these things, my students start changing the form of their work to suit the structure, and that's wrong. They need to honor the organic frame of this beast. This new animal, they have to discover how it breathes. It comes out whole-cloth, and they have to figure out how it lives. They have to figure out the physics of the world in which the beast moves. Every play has its own rules.

In her chapter, Ruhl discusses exercises she finds useful in freeing students from the self-imposed confines of traditional genre conventions, thereby encouraging a greater freedom in the process: "All these things you might learn in graduate school—I think it really tightens us up as writers rather than loosening us. So when you muck around with genre, I think people write more fluidly, and I think plays encompass all genres, like there's the poetry of the speech, there's the argument, which is an essay, there's the story, the spine of it."

These writers consistently encourage their students to think more expansively—to create their own structure. Kron wants them "to want to write better and different from anyone else. I want them to want to 'reinvent' theater so I can feel irritated at them for being so naïve."

But the freeing up of a writer from the potential constriction of convention does not mean that any of these teachers would deny the value of practiced craft or an understanding of how the broad mechanisms serve a play.

Kron writes:

> When I was in my twenties, many people I knew were skeptical of craft, believing it led to formulaic work and canned narratives. They felt its purpose was to stifle wildness, contradiction, and unpredictability. But the old saw is right: real craft is freedom. It's not a map. There's no destination that anyone else can point you toward. It's an intuitive process. But to know theatrical craft is to have the ability to employ our art form's particular mechanisms of dynamic engagement with an audience. If you learn the dynamic principles of dramatic action, and you learn to recognize and manipulate various forms and tropes, you can make something that feels very alive.

In the end, the key is becoming an individual thinker—one who not only forgets the rules and the tricks but also has amassed an array of tools that will truly enable playwrights to write what they want to write.

All the master teachers in this book recognize the potential to learn through studying great plays. Jon Robin Baitz notes, "It's not that you have to have read every play in the canon, it's not even that you have to have read the Poetics—I mean, I am shaky on my Greeks. It's that you must read plays deeply enough so that the epiphany strikes you about their structure or their meaning. It's so much easier for me to talk about other people's plays than it is my own." While playwrights' need to read plays might seem an undisputable point, the fact that these teachers place emphasis on this pursuit perhaps implies that they don't think enough reading—or enough serious reading—of plays is actually undertaken by young writers. Steven Dietz advises study of "how the author is using time to make the narrative come to life. Find the triggering event, the central question, and how the questions we are asking as the audience keep changing and deepening. Underline the unforgettable sentences. See where the short word is. Note how actively the sentence is crafted. Steal the good verbs."

Indeed, most of these teachers advocate strongly for thorough dissection of great works. Quiara Hudes asks her students to come to class prepared after studying a great play and "having listed the different tools that the playwright is using to dramatize his or her story." She writes the tools on the board. "Then, from the tools that they've engaged with the most, I select three tools that they have to go write a play with. Let's say direct address, no stage directions, and the inciting incident is offstage—for instance. They have to go write a ten-page play that uses those tools."

Henley writes that "investing in the deep study of a play, looking at all its elements and all its demands truly broadens [the] ability to think about writing."

Perhaps it might be a matter of borrowing certain elements. Lucas Hnath advocates for "looking at a work that's not your own, poking around, learning something, and transferring that same frame of thinking." It may be that taking the clock apart to see how it ticks enables fresh perspective on one's own mechanism. Within this critical analysis lies the potential to discover for oneself the myriad of approaches that result in powerful drama, a key to developing an individual voice. The act affords inspiration, a playground of available approaches for mirror or juxtaposition.

Speaking from her own experience, Lisa Kron remembers, "The default setting of my Midwestern mind pointed toward linearity and rationality, but over and over again I watched my comrades take aesthetic leaps I was sure were doomed to failure, and was confounded when so much of the time the results were luminous, hilarious, profound, alive. So I try to direct my students toward their own sense of confoundedness and awe."

But true freedom and pursuit of uniqueness clearly implies that teachers must beware the potential impact of creating writers in their own image. As Solis notes, attempts to please the instructor/master writers can be a danger to the creative process. It is not uncommon for this relationship to exist.

Ruhl writes:

> Teaching is tricky. We all know what it is to be, oh, unhinged by power, or not aware of your power. Teaching can be a relationship that's marked by power. And to not notice that I think can be very, very dangerous, especially when you're dealing with art, because it's so vulnerable. You need to have a sense of respect and boundaries around the material that a student's bringing to you.

Carlos Murillo is wary of "putting an aesthetic stamp on my writers or trying to constrain them with received notions about form and content. Our success as a program is best reflected in the wide stylistic bandwidth of work that's come out of it over the years." In an ideal world, notes Murillo, a student's will to write must be "less about external validation and more about an inner drive to solve the mystery of his or her play. Having developed an independent artistry, I become, happily, somewhat redundant to my students."

Inherent in a system that does not promote external validation as a measure of progress is the need for writers to develop measures to promote their own growth. Hudes notes that it is key that writers develop "a process of rigorous self-examination, of learning to critique one's own work lucidly, soberly, to be competitive with oneself."

Hnath writes, "What I've become most interested in is a model of teaching that is about the students identifying what they value and then giving them the tools to assess whether or not their play is matching those values, and if not, what they can do to make the play they want to make."

Learning to promote one's own growth through thoughtful self-reflection is key, but it doesn't negate the value of input from others. Dietz says, "I want them to learn to invite scrutiny." So he .

advises a writer who does not have a ready community able to give feedback to go out and find it:

> What I would say to that playwright who doesn't have that community is this: If you can take a workshop, if you can take a class, if you can find a way, in addition to trying to hear the play, to tell the story of that scene to a friend. Tell the story of that character to a friend. Practice the world of the play. If you have two or three characters in the play, tell me the story of the play in the first person—never use the word "they"—from all their points of view. See what you learn. Ultimately, you as a playwright can read your work aggressively. I think that's when you find your voice.

But the frame through which a writer receives feedback is crucial. First, Ruhl points out that the receipt of feedback should be carefully moderated, noting, "Actually you're not ready for criticism until you've had some nice things said about your work." Within their classrooms, many of these writers advocate for a system of feedback that follows or is based on Liz Lerman's critical response process. It begins with positive feedback.

According to Ruhl, "The audience says what they found meaningful, evocative, striking, and exciting in the work." Then the artist becomes the questioner posing queries that can be answered with yes or no. Then there is an opportunity for questions to the writer but the key is to ask questions that, again according to Ruhl, "do not have an opinion embedded in them." Finally, and only if the writer chooses to do so, opinions on the work can be offered. But permission must be asked for by the "audience" and granted by the writer before these opinions are shared.

Even when a playwright is ready to hear criticism, it is key to provide a perspective that comes from self-evaluation first. Hudes advises: "If one has his or her own process of self-critique, it's a way to stay closer to the work, not let your ideas be blowing through the wind between all the notes and reviews you get."

One of the key points made in this book is the need for writers to take control of the feedback process both to ensure that it is useful and that the feedback received does not derail artistic intention. Lucas Hnath asks his students:

What are you trying to figure out in your play? Can you ask that question in a way that you can get useful feedback in the room? The truth is if they can actually ask the question as an answerable question, I find that the students can answer it for themselves. A lot of playwriting problems—by which I mean playwriting development problems—actually come from not knowing what the question is.

He continues:

Play development becomes play development hell when—this isn't always the case—the playwright hasn't taken control of the process, and the way you take control of it is by telling the people that you're working with—the dramaturg, the artistic director: here's what I'm trying to figure out with this play, and here's how you can help me. Put them to work for you.

Dietz also warns of young writers becoming too dependent on a structure in which only feedback inspires continued work. He worries when students say, "Well, I really want to rewrite it, but I'll do rewrites after I get people's notes," because "rewriting only when you get feedback is problematic." Again, an ability to self-reflect in a way that is useful to the rewriting process is key for all writers.

Finally, Henley ensures that all of her new playwrights "understand that they own the copyright to their play. Any changes they make in a workshop or production need to enhance their vision of the play, and must also belong to them."

Many of these writers stress the idea of surprise and discovery. And it is surprise and discovery for the writer in process that must come first. Henley has found that "true confusion is dramatic and compelling. In drama, it is better not to know the story you are writing. It should evolve out of the pain and search of confusion." Solis wants his students to "approach their writing not through the front door, but through the most unexpected windows." He bemoans that "so many times, we as writers already know what the story is, what's going to happen in it, and how it's going to end." Kron encourages her students to "develop a narrative voice that doesn't know where it's headed, that can only see as far as it can see from where it's standing at a given moment. I encourage them to let go of omniscience, because drama is animated on the opposite of omniscience. Drama utilizes the gap between what people think is happening and what's really happening."

But Kron notes that writing from a place of unknowing—capturing a sense of unknowing within a play when your instinct drives you to know, to plan, to be literal—is extremely difficult. Still, she advocates that this is a key part of the process and writes:

> If you know where you're going when you start, you're not going to get anywhere very interesting, you're going to get wherever you can see from where you're standing at any given moment. [I] try to get [students] to cast around more and surprise themselves and pull things in from all kinds of places and then say at any given moment not "here's where I plan on going," or "here's where I wanted to go all along," but "what is here?" and "what's interesting about it, and what can I do with what's actually here?"

The playwrights in this book all share a deep desire to develop the individual talent that comes before them. As advice to those who teach playwriting, Baitz writes: "In order to teach, you certainly need to have a sense of excitement at the minds of students discovering their own power, their own uniqueness, and their own individual voices. I think it helps to be unsentimental and generously and kindly ruthless while being nurturing."

Murillo strives to "imagine student playwrights as unique organisms in possession of their own distinct, singular voice, sensibility, and way of seeing, waiting to be coaxed out. Perceiving them that way helps me define my job—which is to guide them to write the plays that only they can write." Henley aims to enable them to "discover who they are as artists, to find their singular expression." Baitz continues, "If you are trying to help people find their voice, you are trying to help them find the bravery that it takes to combine everything we have appropriated from outside with what we know from inside and to make words connect to one another, compellingly. It's the bravery—its having an environment in which the voice is as important as the idea."

Octavio Solis writes:

> One of the things that I believe is that every person has at least one important story to tell ... and

if they don't tell it, we will never know it. And no one else will be able to tell that story the way that they do. So I try to impress on them that they should trust their voice to find that one story that must be told their way, and that it is vitally important that it be put it out into the world.

I think the best stories writers can tell are ones that are already inside them, rolled up in the flutes of their bones. It's there. The stories are all there. As long as they write from that special place, they will learn out how potent and dangerous writing can be—and how eternally powerful.

CONTRIBUTOR BIOGRAPHIES

JON ROBIN BAITZ was born in Los Angeles and grew up in Brazil and South Africa. Plays include *Mizlansky/Zilinsky, The Film Society, The Substance of Fire, The End of The Day, Three Hotels, A Fair Country, Ten Unknowns, The Paris Letter, Other Desert Cities*, and *Vicuña*. He is an American Academy of Arts & Letters Award winner, an NEA and Guggenheim fellow, Outer Critics Circle Award winner, and a two-time Pulitzer Prize finalist, first for *A Fair Country,* and most recently for *Other Desert Cities*, for which he was also a Tony-award nominee. For his work in television, he is a GLAD award winner for *Brothers & Sisters*, which ran for five seasons on ABC, and which he created, and a Humanities Award recipient for the PBS TV version of *Three Hotels*. In 2016, his miniseries *The Slap* aired on NBC. He serves on the board of the Ojai Playwrights Conference and is the literary executor of the Lillian Hellman estate.

STEVEN DIETZ's thirty-plus plays and adaptations have been seen at more than one hundred regional theaters in the United States, as well as Off-Broadway. International productions have been seen in more than twenty countries, and his work has been translated into ten languages. Recent world premieres include *Bloomsday* (2016 Steinberg New Play Award Citation); *This Random World* (40th Humana Festival of New American Plays); and *On Clover Road* (NNPN "rolling world premiere"). Other recent work includes *Rancho Mirage* (Edgerton New Play Award), *The Shimmering,* and *American la Ronde.* His two-theater commission of companion plays for adult and young audiences—*The Great Beyond* and *The Ghost of Splinter Cove*—will premiere in 2018.

13

A two-time winner of the Kennedy Center Fund for New American Plays Award *(Fiction, Still Life with Iris),* Dietz is also a two-time finalist for the American Theatre Critic's Steinberg New Play Award *(Last of the Boys, Becky's New Car).* He received the PEN USA West Award in Drama for *Lonely Planet,* and the 2007 Edgar Award for Drama for *Sherlock Holmes: The Final Adventure.* Other widely produced plays and adaptations include *Yankee Tavern, Jackie & Me, Shooting Star, Dracula, Inventing van Gogh, God's Country, Private Eyes,* and *The Nina Variations.*

Mr. Dietz and his family divide their time between Seattle and Austin, where he teaches playwriting and directing at the University of Texas. In addition, he is a Dramatists Guild "Traveling Master," offering playwriting workshops and master classes around the country.

BETH HENLEY was born in Jackson, Mississippi. Her plays have been produced internationally and translated into more than ten languages. *Crimes of the Heart* (the Golden Theatre) and *The Wake of Jamie Foster* (Eugene O'Neill Theatre) were performed on Broadway. Off-Broadway productions include *The Miss Firecracker Contest, Am I Blue, The Lucky Spot, The Debutante Ball, Abundance, Impossible Marriage,* and *Family Week.* Her play *Ridiculous Fraud* was produced at McCarter Theatre as well as South Coast Repertory Theatre.

Ms. Henley's *The Jacksonian* premiered at the Geffen Theatre in January 2012 to great acclaim. Robert Falls directed, and the cast included Ed Harris, Bill Pullman, Amy Madigan, and Glenne Headly. It was performed Off-Broadway at the New Group. Studio Theatre produced the world premier of her newest play, *Laugh,* in 2015, Beth Henley was awarded the Pulitzer Prize in Drama and the New York Drama Critics Circle Award for Best American Play for *Crimes of the Heart.* Other awards include American Theatre Wing 1998 Award for Distinguished Achievement in Playwriting; Susan Smith Blackburn Finalist for *Crimes of the Heart* and *Ridiculous Fraud*; Richard Wright

Literary Excellence Award, 2000; New York Stage and Film Honoree, 2007; ATHE Career Achievement Award, 2010; William Inge Theatre Festival Honoree, 2017.

Ms. Henley has the honor of serving as Theatre Arts Presidential Professor at LMU, Los Angeles. She is a member of the Fellowship of Southern Writers; the Dramatist Guild; and the Academy of Arts and Science.

LUCAS HNATH's plays include *A Doll's House, Part 2*; *Hillary and Clinton*; *Red Speedo*; *The Christians*; *A Public Reading of an Unproduced Screenplay About the Death of Walt Disney*; *Isaac's Eye*; and *Death Tax*. He has been produced on Broadway at the John Golden Theatre, and Off-Broadway at New York Theatre Workshop, Playwrights Horizons, Soho Rep, and Ensemble Studio Theatre. His plays have been produced regionally all over the country with premieres at the Humana Festival of New Plays, Victory Gardens, and South Coast Rep. He has been a resident playwright at New Dramatists since 2011. Awards: Kesselring Prize, Guggenheim Fellowship, Whiting Award, two Steinberg/ATCA New Play Award Citations, Outer Critics Circle Award for Best New Play, and an Obie.

QUIARA ALEGRIA HUDES is the author of a trilogy of plays including *Elliot, A Soldier's Fugue*; *Water By the Spoonful*, and *The Happiest Song Plays Last.* Hudes wrote the book for the Broadway musical *In The Heights*, winner of the Tony Award for Best Musical. Recent work includes the plays *Daphne's Dive* and *The Good Peaches,* and the musical *Miss You Like Hell.* Hudes is the recipient of a Pulitzer Prize for Drama and is the Shapiro Distinguished Professor of Theatre and Writing at Wesleyan University.

LISA KRON is a writer and performer whose work has been widely produced in New York, regionally, and internationally. She wrote the book and lyrics for musical *Fun Home*, with music by composer Jeanine Tesori, which won five 2015 Tony including Best Musical and was finalist for the Pulitzer Prize. Lisa's other plays include *In The Wake*, *Well*, and the Obie-Award winning *2.5 Minute Ride*. As an actor she received a Tony nomination for her performance in *Well* and a Lortel Award for her turn as Mrs. Mi-Tzu and Mrs. Yang in the Foundry Theatre's acclaimed production of *Good Person of Szechwan*. She is the recipient of Guggenheim, Sundance, and MacDowell fellowships, a Doris Duke Performing Artists Award, a Cal Arts/Alpert Award, a Helen Merrill Award, the Kleban Prize for libretto writing, and grants from the Creative Capital and NYFA. Lisa is also founding member of the OBIE- and Bessie-Award-winning collaborative theater company The Five Lesbian Brothers. She serves on the boards of the MacDowell Colony and the Sundance Institute, and is Council Vice President of the Dramatists Guild of America.

CARLOS MURILLO is a Chicago-based playwright of Colombian and Puerto Rican descent. He is a recipient of a 2015 Doris Duke Impact Award and a 2016 Mellon Foundation Playwright Residency at Adventure Stage in Chicago. His body of work has been produced throughout the United States and Europe. His best-known play, *Dark Play or Stories for Boys,* premiered at the Humana Festival at Actors Theatre of Louisville and has been performed throughout the United States, Germany, Poland, Slovakia, Hungary, and Lithuania. The play appeared in the anthology *New Playwrights: Best New Plays of 2007* (Smith & Kraus). His plays have been seen in New York at Repertorio Español, P73, the NYC Summer Playwrights Festival, En Garde Arts, The Public Theatre New Work Now! Festival, and Soho Rep, in Chicago at The Goodman, Steppenwolf, Collaboraction, Walkabout Theatre, Adventure Stage and Theatre Seven, and in Los Angeles at Theatre @ Boston Court, Circle X, and Son of Semele. His plays have been commissioned by Oregon Shakespeare Festival, The Goodman, the Public Theatre, Playwrights Horizons, Berkeley Rep, South Coast Rep, Steppenwolf, and Adventure Stage, and developed by The Sundance Theatre Lab, The Playwrights' Center, the Bay Area Playwrights Festival, New Dramatists, and others. The Javier Plays, a trilogy of works including *Diagram of a Paper Airplane, A Thick Description of Harry Smith*, and

Your Name Will Follow You Home is published by 53rd State Press. His other work is published by Dramatists Play Service, Broadway Play Publishing, and Dramatic Publishing. Awards include the Met Life Nuestros Voces Award from Repertorio Español, the Frederick Loewe Award from New Dramatists, the Ofner Prize from the Goodman Theatre, the Otis Guernsey Award from the William Inge Theatre Festival, a Jerome Fellowship at The Playwrights' Center, and two National Latino Playwriting Awards from Arizona Theatre Company. Carlos heads the BFA Playwriting Program at the Theatre School of DePaul University and is a proud alumnus of New Dramatists. Carlos lives in Chicago with his wife, the director Lisa Portes, and their two children Eva and Carlitos.

SUZAN-LORI PARKS: The Public Theatre: *Father Comes Home from the Wars* (Parts 1, 2 & 3) (Pulitzer Prize finalist), *Watch Me Work, The Book of Grace, 365 Days/365 Plays* (in conjunction with more than seven hundred theaters worldwide), *Topdog/ Underdog, Fucking A, In the Blood* (Pulitzer Prize finalist), *Venus, The America Play*. Broadway: *The Gershwins' Porgy and Bess, Topdog/Underdog*. Other Off-Broadway productions include *Unchain My Heart, The Death of the Last Black Man in the Whole Entire World ...,* and *Imperceptible Mutabilities in the Third Kingdom*. Film includes *Girl 6* (directed by Spike Lee), *Their Eyes Were Watching God* (produced by Oprah Winfrey), and *Anemone Me* (produced by Christine Vachon and Todd Haynes). Suzan-Lori is the first African-American woman to receive the Pulitzer Prize in Drama. She is a MacArthur Fellowship ("Genius" Grant) recipient. Other awards include the Tony Award for Best Revival of a Musical (*Porgy and Bess),* the Gish Prize for Excellence in the Arts, Edward M. Kennedy Prize for Drama, Horton Foote Prize, and the Obie Award for *Playwriting: Best New American Play*. Suzan-Lori teaches at New York University and serves at the Public Theatre as its Master Writer Chair. She also currently performs *Watch Me Work*, a free, live-streamed, weekly writing workshop, open to artists of all disciplines. Her first novel, *Getting Mother's Body* (Random House, 2003), includes songs and is set in the West

Texas of her youth. She has recently written a screen adaptation of Richard Wright's *Native Son*, a new screenplay about Billie Holiday, two new stage plays, and a musical adaptation of the film *The Harder They Come*. She fronts her band Suzan-Lori Parks and The Band. For more info, visit SuzanLori Parks.com.

SARAH RUHL's plays include *How to Transcend a Happy Marriage; For Peter Pan on her 70th Birthday; The Oldest Boy; In the Next Room, or the Vibrator Play; The Clean House; Orlando, Late: A Cowboy Song; Dear Elizabeth;* and *Stage Kiss*. She is a two-time Pulitzer Prize finalist and a Tony Award nominee. Her plays have been produced on Broadway at the Lyceum by Lincoln Center Theatre, and off-Broadway at Playwrights Horizons, Second Stage, and at Lincoln Center's Mitzi Newhouse Theatre. Her plays have been produced regionally all over the country, produced internationally, and translated into more than twelve languages. Ms. Ruhl received her MFA from Brown University where she studied with Paula Vogel. She has received the Steinberg Distinguished Playwright award; the Susan Smith Blackburn award; the Whiting award; the Lily Award; a PEN award for mid-career playwrights; and the MacArthur Fellowship. Her book of essays, *100 Essays I Don't Have Time to Write,* was published by Faber and Faber last fall. She teaches at the Yale School of Drama and lives in Brooklyn with her family.

OCTAVIO SOLIS is a playwright and director whose works *Alicia's Miracle, Se Llama Cristina,* John Steinbeck's *The Pastures of Heaven, Ghosts of the River, Quixote, Lydia, June in a Box, Lethe, Marfa Lights, Gibraltar, The Ballad of Pancho and Lucy, The 7 Visions of Encarnacion, Bethlemen, Dreamlandia, El Otro, Man of the Flesh, Propsect, El Paso Blue, Santos & Santos,* and *La Posada Magica* have been mounted at the California Shakespeare Theatre, Mark Taper Forum, Yale Repertory Theatre, the Oregon Shakespeare Festival, the Denver Center for the Performing Arts, the Dallas Theatre Center, the Magic Theatre, Intersection for the Arts, South Coast Repertory Theatre, the San Diego Repertory Theatre, Shadowlight Productions, the Venture Theatre in Philadelphia, Theatre at Boston Court, the Kitchen

Dog Theatre, Teatro Vista, El Teatro Campesino, the Undermain Theatre, Thick Description, Campo Santo, INTAR, and Cornerstone Theatre. His collaborative works include *Cloudlands,* with music by Adam Gwon, and *Shiner*, written with Erik Ehn. Solis has received an NEA 1995–97 Playwriting Fellowship, the Kennedy Center's Roger L. Stevens Award, the Will Glickman Playwright Award, the 1998 TCG/NEA Theatre Artists in Residence Grant, the 1998 McKnight Fellowship grant from the Playwrights Center in Minneapolis, and the National Latino Playwriting Award for 2003. He is the recipient of the 2000–01 National Theatre Artists Residency Grant from TCG and the Pew Charitable Trust, the United States Artists Fellowship for 2011, and the 2104 Pen Center USA Award for Drama. Solis is a Thornton Wilder Fellow for the MacDowell Colony, a New Dramatists alum, and member of the Dramatists Guild.

MAC WELLMAN's recent work includes *The Offending Gesture*, directed by Meghan Finn at the Connelly Theater in 2016; *Horrocks (and Toutatis Too)* and *Woo World Wu* at Emerson College in Boston in 2013 (with Erin Mallon & Tim Sirgusa); *Muazzez* at the Chocolate Factory (PS122's COIL Festival) with Steve Mellor, in 2014; *3 2's; or AFAR* at Dixon Place in October 2011, *The Difficulty of Crossing a Field* (with composer David Lang) at Montclair in the fall of 2006 (and elsewhere more recently); and *1965 UU* for performer Paul Lazar, and directed by Stephen Mellor at the Chocolate Factory in the fall of 2008. He has received numerous honors, including NEA, Guggenheim, and Foundation of Contemporary Arts fellowships. In 2003 he received his third Obie, for Lifetime Achievement. In 2006 his third novel, *Q's Q*, was published by Green Integer, and in 2008 a volume of stories, *A Chronicle of the Madness of Small Worlds*, was published by Trip Street Press as well as a new collection of plays, *The Difficulty of Crossing a Field*, from Minnesota Press. His books of poetry include *Miniature* (2002), *Strange Elegies* (2006), *Split the Stick* (2012) from Roof Books, and *Left Glove* (2011) from Solid Objects Press. His novel *Linda Perdido* won the 2011 FC2 Catherine Doctorow Prize for Innovative Fiction. He is Distinguished Professor of Play Writing at Brooklyn College.

Jon Robin Baitz

I began caring about theater because it was familiar to me because I lived so much more in imagination more than the real world as a kid. I was probably the last person to stop playing cops and robbers games. In fact, I probably never did stop. All those plots about justice and right and wrong. I loved going to the theater from an early age and found myself much happier in a movie theater or a regular theater. In my early twenties, going to the theater became a much bigger part of my life. Los Angeles, in the early 1980s, was quite fecund theatrically. There was a lot to see. You could go several nights a week, if you wanted, and I did.

There is a certain kind of person for whom the theater means more than the movies because proximity tells you more—proximity to the actor, proximity to the artifice made real, the melding of make believe and ritual with psychological truth. In that way, the stage becomes a more useful frame through which to view the world. I started to feel that it was becoming more magical for me, more powerful for me—what the proscenium would do—what the space would do. And, of course, I thought a great deal about the kinds of stories being told in the theater.

I fell in with a now defunct playwrights' conference, the Padua Hills Playwrights Festival. The storytelling was quite often unconventional. Originally, the plays were site specific. I saw an Irene Fornes play, *Mud*. This was the first production of the play. And the outside world took on all the qualities that a stage had, which was extraordinary. Parts of the festival were workshops, a day with these master playwrights. I think, during one of my first little bits of playwriting, I spent a page doing stage description.

Irene said, in that sort of high-pitched Cuban accent, "If you do that much stage description: a), you become nervous about starting writing, and b), no one else has any oxygen in which to create." It was a tiny quip, a tiny comment, but it stuck with me. Like any good lesson, it had a larger context to it. The playwright's job was, in some ways, to do as little as is needed in order to set the world moving. That's how it all started.

I think there are many qualities that are valuable for playwrights to bring to the table and others that can be more easily taught. Playwrights need to learn how to identify a sense of the undercurrent beneath the literal world. Why a moment is so important that it needs to be written. It's important for playwrights to discern the code under the dialogue—that they were writing toward something, even if it was subconsciously. I work without much conscious understanding at any given moment. But I think that knowingness is important—the knowing that there is an urgency underneath or that there is a fear underneath or that people aren't necessary telling the truth. It's an almost instinctual skill: The hunting of the lie.

An ear helps. It's hard to be a good playwright if you don't understand the musicality of human speech—if you don't understand that there are rhythms, and that words arranged together in a certain order create a kind of musicality that becomes a concerto or a symphony or a partita, depending on how you use them. The instincts regarding musicality are important for playwrights to develop.

The things you can teach are forward movement, the question of how a plot advances, that what's going to happen next must always be part of your process. A complicated play like *The Cryptogram* by David Mamet is filled with ellipses, filled with mystery, filled with opacity. But it's also terribly, terribly urgent. So as a teacher of playwriting – if you are a decent practitioner of it – you want to pry open doors for students to help them develop the skills they need to open the next door.

You can teach editing. You can teach them to use as few words a possible or to use as many words as possible depending on the moment. I don't assign many exercises in my class, but I do have a few—one of which focuses on economy of language: write a scene between two characters where one explains why they are leaving, perhaps never to come back, while packing. Then rewrite that scene but cut it in half, doing the same thing. You can use the bones of the scene you first wrote and simply edit it down to halve its length and see what remains. See how few words it takes to tell the truth you're telling. Try it even again, a third time, and see what's left. Keep going until there's virtually nothing left on the page and then start over.

You can teach them how a stage is both a room, a photograph, while also being a lens through which you are seeing something you're not supposed to see. All of those things can be sort of accumulated.

They can learn by being around you, by watching you talk about their plays, and their peer's plays. Having a semester-long or however-many-hours-long conversations about the theater that takes place naturally during seminars is key. In being critical of their work, you're teaching them about the notions that sparked you and why. So the back and forth of it, the familiarity part of it is crucial.

I have taught BFA and MFA students. I started as a playwright—professionally very young, at twenty-four—but that's harder now. Just to become a professional playwright with no formal training, its harder to get access to theatres as a young playwright. When I started there were a lot of "amateurs." You could talk your way in, or show some pages to an artistic director. I wonder if the culture or the climate somehow places emerging playwrights in a kind of stasis, or limbo, waiting for the approval of teachers, rather than emerging themselves like say, a rock band might, out of a garage.

I worry about the hesitancy to embrace conditions on the ground – fostered by the schools. I was teaching in a BFA class in UC San Diego, and I assigned *Hedda Gabler* to read. I remember talking about it, and one of the students hadn't bothered reading because he read it in high school. And I said, "But the point is, you're not the person you were in high school. You are not in high school and we read the gauge where we now are, especially re-reading with new understanding, works that had fewer resonances when we were younger." This had to be pointed out.

Undergrads may not have been given—and this is such a generalization—given how weird it is to grow up now—may not have had enough time to figure out basic life stuff. They spend so much goddamn time trying to get into university, it's like they're still in fight-or-flight syndrome. School should be a four-year conversation about what it means to be alive. So maybe it's better if they've lived a little more before having to interpret it for the sake of a BFA or something. Besides, I always tell people who are going to college to study anything but writing, like art history or microeconomics or how to build trains.

By the time you get to grad school, it's not that you necessarily know more, but you're far abler to accept that you don't know as much as you once thought you did. It's a much better moment to teach. Of course, paradoxically, as I said, I started really young and I didn't go to school at all.

In order to teach, you certainly need to have a sense of excitement regarding the minds of students discovering their own power, their own uniqueness, and their own individual voices. I think it helps to be unsentimental and generously and kindly ruthless while being nurturing. Those are acquired skills. When I started teaching, I had no idea what any of it was made of, and I thought it was enough to do my show—sort of a Lenny Bruce, Saul Bellow, Andy Warhol, John Waters, Phyllis Diller combo pack. And eventually you just need only to be more … you.

The first task is to understand their goal, to understand where they are in their development as a writer, and not project onto them the thing you want but to listen to what they think they need. In some cases, it's simply the ability to write a full-length play, sustain a narrative over eighty or 120 minutes because sometimes when you get students, they really haven't written that many full-length plays and it's a newer skill. It's not that it's easier to write a shorter play, it's just that it's got a different set of dynamics to it, just engineering-wise.

The first few weeks of my classes are almost just talk—talking about our experience in the theater, the things that have meant something to us, of our own histories in as much as one is willing to share, the things that compel you politically, historically, sociologically, the reasons for being there. It's to try to ascertain what their expectations are and what has moved them and why. It's often a case of people coming into class with a work in progress and wanting to see it though, or if not that, a student with fermenting ideas of a play and helping him or her find the starting point. There's a period of discovery.

At a certain point, Michael Feingold wrote about me that I was endlessly and singularly obsessed with the stories about parents and children, and it wasn't a compliment. For a moment it sort of stung, and then I thought, actually, if I am it's because I'm really compelled by the questions of how we become who we are going to be as individuals. Our first world is that of our family oftentimes. I can't help but be drawn to it as much as I am or have been in the past.

You can't outgrow something just because someone at the Village Voice, for instance, wants you to. The playwrights' trajectory is to recognize why they are interested in the world. That is the most important thing you can teach. Playwrights must be able to ask themselves the why of their obsession, of their curiosity.

We talk about character. All characters have secrets. The question is, are the secrets relevant to the story? If you can articulate the useful secrets, the useful secrets will unlock the next door of a play for you. The useless secrets might be just as important. Everybody needs to remember that the only thing that makes sense is a mysterious process where doors are locked and there is an infinite number of doors until there are very few left. But they might not see the last few doors in this house, in this room, in this tunnel. If you keep asking questions, if they're the right types of questions, this unlocks the door. Sometimes this is accelerated. If you write a play very quickly, this is accelerated. But sometimes you may reverse-engineer the play. The doors are still there.

The one thing I know about playwriting is this: "Character is fate," which is the foundation of drama. It's from Heraclitus: "A man's character is his fate." And what is character? It's just the choices we make that reveal our moral purpose. That's like basic Aristotle, right? Our character determines our fate, so a play can tell you about itself. Sometimes it takes longer than it reasonably should be. Sometimes you even need other people to read it, because you're too close to it. It always helps to have someone very, very smart, usually a director that you have a relationship with, an experienced director who can help you. Where is the seam of character and fate intersecting, etc.—not in any schematic way. It may be mysterious or it may be obvious—i.e., Richard Nixon may have been really smart and had a few good ideas here and there (though I am not sure, other than understanding that China mattered, what they were), but his character—mistrusting, vindictive, paranoid, small—well, that character determined his fate. Donald Trump's fate will be defined by his character, and if I were teaching now, the students would be writing about the president all the time.

The notion of building the play is pretty arbitrary for me. I don't know much about outlining plays. In my case it's never been a very useful methodology. I can't think of a play that I've outlined. I've known endings. I've known what something ends up as, and you don't know how to get there. But I think it's organic. At a certain point, if you're like me and you're not great at plot, plot becomes very important. If your right knee is injured, you end up using your left knee quite a bit, and your left knee starts to hurt through over-use. If you're good at character but not plot and you know that, you become very interested in the way plot works. You find the thing you are weakest at and you sort of make character teach you about plot. I'm terrible at plot. It's why I write plays that actually have them. I overcompensate for my bad weak knee.

We talk about the writer's voice, and the question of voice really is a large question. It's about confidence. If you're trying to help people find their voice, you're trying to help them find the bravery that it takes to combine everything we have appropriated from outside with what we know from inside and make words connect to one another compellingly. It's the bravery—its having an environment in which the voice is as important as the idea. What's your idea? How do you live in your idea? Asking those kinds of questions leads to people being able to look at differentiating their characters' voices, I think.

We face writers' block. Anyone who says they have an answer for that is misleading others. Writers' block is just too different from person to person. Writers' block has different reasons. You can't confuse being a person who teaches playwriting with being some sort of therapist. I have no answers about writers' block. In my case, it has to do with fighting depression all my life and fighting the terror of starting a thing that I know is going to take a lot out of me—a thing that is going to take a lot of time to get right. It's a big commitment. Writers' block maybe is a form of phobia about committing. You can't help someone with stasis. Sometimes terror helps. Sometimes the act of having a deadline in a class is enough to get something happening. I just think writers' block is an inevitability. I would be very suspicious of a teacher who said he or she can help you through that.

The fundamental A, B, and C that I teach is that you must be able to write dramatically and not polemically. I once had a very famous writer in a workshop of mine—she wasn't a playwright. She was a renowned writer of women's issues and sociological impacts on women and aging and sex, and she was trying to write a play that was somewhat autobiographical. But because she had also been a journalist and a reporter, she came in with the mistaken notion that her memory of events would lead her to be able to transcribe those events in a way that other people found compelling. So what she came in with was flat and inarticulate in the muscular sense—it didn't have tautness to it. These are fundamentals that separate drama from polemicism and didacticism. That's the ABCs.

I often assign a particular play to read and talk about. The plays I have them read are always changing. I like people to read Pinter plays because he has evolved so much as a playwright, and he's a brilliant editor of the self. From the shortest plays of his, like *Mountain Language* and *One for the Road*, to the great giant ones, there is so much precision. It's not that I'm obsessed with Harold Pinter; it's just that they're really wonderful plays to read. They become less oblique in certain places. If you look at a play like *The Birthday Party* and then *Betrayal*, there's a kind of willingness to commit a crime on the page. I like Stoppard because no playwright I can think of has been more willing to embrace the urgency of our interior intellectual life with as much easy fluid grace, in some ways. Chekhov is endlessly confusing, and that's a kind of really good person to have around. Those are plays that are rich because they infuriate people, people shrug at them, people become enamored and obsessed with them, people identify with them, they misidentify with them, they misunderstand them. They attach themselves to them. You can take a play like *The Seagull* and spend a semester poking at it and learn a lot. It's a matter of being a good reader of plays, that's all.

Say it's *The Tempest*, for instance. We can talk about power and enslavement and sexual roles and masters and servants and revenge. Perhaps you might talk about *Cherry Orchard* and we can talk about our understanding of what it means to ignore the obvious conditions around you that are hastening your own demise and how we relate to that. How can a play that takes place in Russia over a hundred years ago resonate so exquisitely today? We can look at the element of revenge in that play and how does that connect to the element of revenge in *The Tempest*.

What is revenge in theater? What does revenge mean? What does it mean to breathe? What does it mean to walk? The questions become about how we live our lives and how the living life relates to the writing life. David Hare's plays are really interesting to me because they speak of people and of the character of a nation. He's always poking at the scene of the crime—take *Skylight*—which is gorgeous in it is enormously relevant to the effects of Thatcherite England on its populace while also looking right at one very particular little love story. There's so much conflict in it—maybe by "crime," I actually mean conflict? I believe in a moral order; I just don't think there really is one.

Maybe we're looking at structure. Wally Shawn's gorgeous play *The Designated Mourner* doesn't pay that much attention to the conventional rules of action on a stage. But there's a kind of magic by which a spell is cast. Always on stage a spell is being cast. And the fundamental skill is to learn how to cast that spell. In the case of *The Designated Mourner*, it's through a deeply serious invocation of horror that also manages to be simultaneously frightening, funny, and recognizable.

You can read a play like *The Pillowman*, which is beautifully inventive, and then actually see a great production of it. It helps if you can take them to see *Endgame* after having read it. If you can expose people to the link between the word on the page and the production, that goes a long way, I think. And help talk about the transition from one to the other. Reading and seeing is very much a part of the theater experience.

I remember when I started reading plays, and I would hear them in my head, and they were perfect. And then I might go see a production of a play I'd read, and it was utterly imperfect, but it was probably more alive because you have to start learning what actors and lights and sets do to ideas. A lot of this teaching stuff is about immersion in a culture of theater. I think in order to be a playwright you have to have some idea of why you're interested in the strange thing you happen to be interested in.

Why does Annie Baker, for instance, keep writing plays in which silence and the measure between the lines is so compelling? What is

Annie doing in a play like *The Flick*, which seems to unspool in real time before your eyes? Why is she interested in filling that space that unspools before your eyes? Why is she interested in that recreation onstage of the banality of everyday life? What compels her? Well, Annie is probably asking all sorts of questions about the undercurrents between our words and our actions. I suppose the recognition of cultural literacy of some sort—to know that which you don't know—is probably the most important fundamental ABC: to know that there are vast areas to learn about when writing.

As an aside: I also think playwrights need great directors who really hear them in ways they can't hear themselves. In Annie's case, to some extent, there is Sam Gold, who uses her pages like a conductor uses sheet music to create a kind of glorious sound. In my case it's been Dan Sullivan and Joe Mantello, who insist on specificity and order in a way that stimulates me to provide those things.

If you are, say, Steven Karam, and you're writing about the nature of our suffering and our bravery, every day in some way is spent stuck in your fundamental philosophy—where do you find kindness? Where do you find honor? I'm talking specifically about Steven. What does it mean to be stoic? What does it mean to have secrets that can cause demons to arise? You have to find your nature as a playwright. In David Hare's case, is he looking between the discrepancy between our public lives and our private lives? Yes, he is, and he is compelled by the combination of our inner selves and our secret policies within, and how they interact with the structures of a society that are usually terribly unfair. It's very helpful to know why you are who you are. Why you are obsessed with certain sorrows—in the case of Sam Shepard—a lost masculinity, a lost west, a lost father, a lost love—loss.

What does it mean if you want to write a play about Mark Rothko and his assistant? What are we saying, really, about the creative act as a writer, say in the case of John Logan with *Red*? The ceaseless brutality and mystery of creativity. You can tell yourselves that things are interesting. You can say, "I want to write a play about something, but that is not enough." Take a successful play like *Frost/Nixon.* The pleasure of the play is not simply in its appropriation of interviews but in the playwright having known his version of the conversations off camera and having been confident enough in his capability as a dramatist to make those really compelling. Why? You have to figure out. It's not that the why exists in a vacuum—you figure out why to figure out how.

It's not that you have to have read every play in the cannon. It's not even that you have to have read the Poetics—I mean, I'm shaky on my Greeks. It's that you must read plays deeply enough so that the epiphany strikes you about their structure or meaning. It's so much easier for me to talk about other people's plays than my own.

My advice is to go to as much theater and read as many plays as you can. Make friends with actors. Love actors. Write for actors. Write for actors some more. Learn their quirks and love them for them. The wonderful thing about being a playwright is that you can get some friends together and do a little show for your other friends. That's a good way to look at it. To start it. It is an art that rewards the amateur.

The truth is there aren't many exercises that make sense to me. Writing a play makes sense to me. As an exercise, write a play that takes place first in a café, then in the hat check room of a restaurant while people are waiting for their coats. Write a scene where both of those people are alone at the end—those are three scenes. The last scene probably has no words. So I might construct ways in which there are parameters to write a short play.

I don't know if that's useful, but it's arbitrary and demanding and works like a little stress test on the nerves of a playwright—come up with something that has a trajectory within the narrow parameters I describe. Frankly, exercises seem like running track to me—go 'round and 'round on a field again and again but get stronger and faster while doing it. That said, I'm not big on them, unless someone is not getting something and you can create an exercise that addresses the particular problem.

Sometimes I ask a student who is stuck in a particularly gnarled knotted ball of a problem to rewrite the scene in the form of a letter from each character to the other, thereby taking it out of the world of necessary dialogue and into a more psychological one where you are weirdly empowered by description. Then you can take those two letters and translate them in some way, with as few words as possible, into the scene you're having trouble with.

A sketch can become a play if there's enough echo in it. So that is something to try and use exercises to convey. What you thought might have just been a tiny, tiny moment, observed or imaged, might just be the Polaroid still of a film that you have yet to make on stage. Then you have them work on it.

One of the interesting byproducts of an engaging MFA education is that it can teach you about community. For instance, if you've been a loner, to some extent you learn how to talk to other writers, to your peers, so the discussion of other people's work, finding ways to encourage them is a helpful form of honesty. This might simply consist of the response to the first round of an exercise—asking questions about the piece rather than making proclamations—and that might move on to a second round in which, without being proscriptive, you share impressions of what actually was happening. All this is interrogative of the playwright.

Collaboration is essential. At the New School, where I taught for six years or so, there's a program called co-lab that puts the writers, directors, and actors together to create new work. It's probably the most useful invention for organically doing a simulation of the process outside school. So co-lab is good. It's also chaos because inexperienced actors are inexperienced in a different way from inexperienced writers. And inexperienced directors are very different from inexperienced actors and writers, so it can be incredibly chaotic, which requires a lot of refereeing by the professors. In the case of co-lab, there is a playwright (me), a directing professor, and an acting professor. You try to create these teams where there are people at different levels of experience, if not organic talent.

Working on new plays is just like life; you're going to lose some and you're going to win some and you're going to find yourself influenced by, for instance, more experienced directors. In my case, I have certainly deferred at times, sometimes much to the betterment of the play. And sometimes things are lost. It is, basically, experience. It's a question of experience. You lose stuff and you learn from your mistakes. It's really important to have a lot of mistakes as a playwright. My shows that have not worked out as well have taught me a lot more than the ones that have. One things I learned from a play that worked really well—my most successful play, *Other Desert Cities*—was when my director, Joe Mantello, told me, "You think you're finished but you're not. You won't be finished until it opens." You have to be open to input. I always say about myself, "I know what words to write, but I'm not quite sure where to put them."

That's my struggle. Some people, for instance, look at my plays and like them because they're arranged. But I often don't know how to arrange the play. I can't tell you how many times I've sat with a director, who says, "Yes, that's wonderful, that bit of writing, that block of writing. If you just moved A to B and B to A, this would create much more sense for you."

My brain does not flow logically. It flows in breaks and starts and cataclysms and distaste, in shutters and burps and breaks and fractures. I'm a bit psychologically unorganized. So if people reading this like my plays, they should understand that I had a little bit of help along the way.

The large question for me is about this community of theater people that you're trying to get to come together to learn. When I started working as a playwright, it wasn't necessarily incumbent upon a playwright to enter into the craft professionally. You could wander into it; you could come at it from another place. There wasn't necessarily an education in it available, and programs like Yale's and Juilliard's, for instance, just to name two successful programs, were one way in; now those programs are, in many cases, one of the only ways in. Part of this is because of the economics of the theater now. If you take a look at development at regional theaters across the country, young playwrights' workshops—let's say a Latina writers workshop, let's say an African-American writers workshop that draws from communities—those are underfunded now. Those have been whittled away. That is slowly changing, thank God.

In many cases a writer who may have come out of a particular community, let's say it was a writer from the Mark Taper Forum, for example, now doesn't have that opportunity. The cutting of all of those programs nationally, the cutting of funding for the arts has meant that in many cases, getting an MFA in playwriting is the path to a career. But paradoxically, those programs can become very expensive and laden a playwright with over $100,000 or even more in debt. So something fundamental has to change in the way that playwrights are given opportunities to rise up professionally, and through communities. Probably through scholarships and even summer programs.

I'm really involved in the Ojai playwrights conference, and I spent this summer with a number of playwrights at various points in their career, most actually just starting, who came to work on plays at the Ojai conference. Some were given scholarships because of the avidity of supporters of the festival wanting to support important new work, especially work by minorities. That's a way in. I don't know, but I think at Yale and Juilliard the students don't pay; they're given full freight. That has to be the way it works. Learning to become a playwright shouldn't be that expensive, I think.

Through teaching, I think I've learned to be able to analyze and articulate the things that I see perhaps more clearly than I would if I were by myself. I've learned that I'm not necessarily made for teaching and that it requires a kind of generosity of spirit that I don't possess in as much abundance as required. I feel like I am stealing from myself, time wise, when I do it. What keeps me doing it is the excitement of being around new voices. It's mostly a matter of learning how to express ideas and communicate. It hasn't made me a better playwright. Nothing will make me a better playwright except writing a play.

My best moment in teaching is very easy to talk about: the emergent voice being realized. It is the moments where a playwright has a kind of success outside the classroom that validates the process. It's when they go on to do things they were going to do anyway … but you've at least been part of their trajectory.

STEVEN DIETZ

I came to playwriting through directing. I lied my way into being a director at the Playwrights' Center in Minneapolis. This would be like 1980–81, around the time that Lee Blessing, August Wilson, all these amazing playwrights were arriving and starting to do their work at the Center. I had written one bad one-act play in college, because I was frankly too arrogant or lazy to actually read a bunch of one-act plays for my directing class. So I wrote a bad one and directed it. My orientation was, and is, as a director, and that's how I made my living the first ten years or so of my career. I was constantly directing readings and workshops of new plays at the Playwrights' Center, and at some point I was working on new plays so regularly that by osmosis I think my own curiosity made me want to start writing plays on my own. So I was writing them as early as 1981–82, though my playwriting career didn't really begin in earnest until the late '80s. To this day I consider myself a director who writes plays.

I teach in one of the big MFA playwriting programs, the University of Texas at Austin. I do this despite never getting my own MFA. In fact, I have never taken a playwriting class. I got hands-on learning instead, and I try to be very candid with my students about the differences in those models. Directing a new play for what seemed like every single week at the Playwrights' Center was my boot camp, my education, my grad school. UT/Austin was my first full-time teaching job. I had done master classes at theaters and universities around the country for twenty-something years, but I'd never been part of a university program. UT created this position in 2005 and I started in 2006. I'm twelve years in, teaching primarily the MFA playwrights and directors.

Something I assume as a teacher: none of us is writing as well as we want. I'm not. I'm not writing as well as I want, or I want to write a little bit better, or there's a play I'm trying to write that I haven't figured out how to write yet because I think, *I'll just do it like that other play that worked!* That, of course, is a fool's errand. There's no shortcut. There's no template. There's no secret. I wish there was. I've been looking for it for thirty years. So through my teaching I hope to complicate your thinking. I'm hoping I can just throw a little stone in the water and let some of these thoughts ripple out for you.

At UT, I teach a playwriting workshop and I teach a class on time as a narrative strategy. I teach a class on story-making for the stage. I teach a collaboration class. The core principle in all of those classes is what I would call the Living Play, which centers on how we go about making the event in the room alive—continually alive—for our audience. I find the heart of this in story-making. I don't teach the well-made play, nor do I teach from a template. I believe the principals of the Living Play are central to any kind of narrative: traditional, experimental, etc.

My students come in saying, "I want to get better at telling a story," just as I did when I was a young playwright hoping my colleagues and audiences wouldn't call me out on the massive gaps in my narrative playmaking. Story has the biggest seat in the room. And I try to come at it from a slightly different angle—perhaps as a conscious disruption, perhaps because it feels organic to me. I don't teach plot or character or action or theme. I find these words inert and spineless. I teach what I consider to be the three central tenets of the Living Play: Motion, Status, and Time.

The reason I teach Motion is that I don't think plays need "action" (as typically understood). I hope that's heresy. Let me say it this way: I describe action as "things happening." There's this myth that our play will be alive and engaging if enough things are happening. I don't find that to be true. Yes, things should happen in your play. Please make things happen in your play—but there is only narrative engagement in your play when something *changes*. The reason I teach motion is that I would call action "things happening" and I would call motion "things changing." I feel my job is to remind students that something in the play—moment to moment to moment, page by page—is changing, deepening, complicating, transforming. I spend a lot of time with students exploring what I've taken to calling "horizontal motion" (external, tangible, observed) and "vertical motion" (internal, emotional, felt). Both of them change the play in the moment, whether there is some "action" happening or not.

I teach Status instead of character because I believe status is what brings a character to life. Status is essentially the power shifts between characters onstage. Who's in power? Is that power implied, assumed, or created? What's the gristle between characters? What is being either explicitly or implicitly negotiated? Too much talk about character centers on independent traits: well, he's twenty-six, he works at Google, he likes to go to the Tigers games, whatever. Those are independent traits, and that may give the actor a few signposts, but narratively it gives me nothing. A character isn't someone I invent; it is someone I make impact something or someone. By making a list of independent traits, I haven't done anything yet. Status makes me look at *inter*dependent traits. What does that character need or fear from that other character? Where is the gap in that character's makeup? What is the power dynamic between those characters? Equal status—or unchanging status—between characters will kill a story very quickly. The shifting power between my characters is central to the work of my play.

As we sit here today: What are the traits of Joan? What are the traits of Dietz? Those are independent traits about you and me and gosh they are neat, but nothing is happening in our scene! As soon as we put our status with each other front and center—instead of our "character traits"—we might get a little something happening.

1. I know a secret about you, Joan.
2. Actually you don't, Dietz—I talked to your wife last night. There's something she wants me to tell you.

Our relationship is shifting and therefore alive. Status is a way to keep a quickening in a relationship. Why is there so much happening in a Chekhov play even though they are just sitting in those chairs? Status is why. Power is being negotiated. A playwright's job is to disrupt people. Disrupt relationships. Disrupt expectations. The story lives in the disruptions.

Rather than plot or even structure (though I'm a nut for structure), I teach Time as a narrative strategy. That is probably my most well-known class at UT. I really don't think I've ever used the word plot in twelve years—maybe because all I see in my head when I hear that word is a big gray battleship that is impermeable and dull as shit. Instead I talk about how we frame a play with time and how we make time function in a way that ignites our story. My own plays have shown me that every problem is structural. Rather than apply some borrowed structure that will fit my story inside a box that looks like a play, I am trying to aggressively take the play to where the story resides most resonantly in Time.

The Greeks had two kinds of time: *kronos* and *kairos*. Kronos is tick-tick-tick-tick—like my watch ticking right now. Chronological time. But *kairos* is different and special. Kairos is the *opportune moment*. What is the moment when your life changed? What is the point of no return? Sometimes I'll put the timeline of my own life on the board for students and mark the *kairos* moments—the watershed moments. Those will include my marriage, the birth of my daughter, the adoption of my son, the death of my dad, the time I almost drowned in that pool in Akron, Colorado, when I was eight. There are, of course, huge gaps between these few large events. What's all that stuff in between? As a student of mine once beautifully said, "You were probably just eating sandwiches."

So the dullest parts of the play are usually when—time-wise—the characters are just eating sandwiches. We don't need to watch people eat sandwiches! The *kairos* moments, the opportune moments are what we seek. Our work with time teaches us how to stack/sequence/place these moments against the audience's innate narrative expertise. The same exact moment is completely different on page eight than it is on page eighty—and that's because the audience is hardwired to a narrative brain that knows an early surprise is a setup but a late surprise is a payoff. Or to put it another way: "Late has weight." So what will you put late in your play, despite where it may have happened chronologically in the character's life?

And where will you come in? Where will you start the play? In my experience (both teaching and with my own plays), this is a bigger question than most people think. We don't start the play with, "Romeo and Juliet were born. They were swaddled as babies." Right? Or "Willy Loman just got his first job as a salesman." The aggressiveness of coming in *right before* all hell breaks loose is apt and refreshing and unforgettable. (Showing a line on the table) I mean *Death of Salesman*, if this is Willy's story, *Death of a Salesman* starts here (marking a spot very near the end of the line). It starts right here. The story-making question isn't *who* is Willy Loman. It's *when* is Willy Loman? Put him in Time and you know the man. "I am back from my last trip." If I'm Miller, I lead with that, and then I go back and get what I need from earlier in Willy's life, because if I don't go back and get that Boston hotel room scene, I don't have a way out of this play. "You're a fraud, Dad."

Again, the chronology of the actual events is meaningless. I don't owe any fealty to that chronologically. I take the play to the story. I get into the play late. I go back and get what I need. The adage of mine my students likely quote the most is: "The past is a burning house." So when we go to the past in a play, go in, get what you want, get the potent stuff, get the hell out. Bring me back to what will now be a changed present.

Let me be the first to say that none of these are secrets, none of these are new ideas, but the organizing principle of my teaching is about learning and exploring active strategies. Time is a great way to keep a quickening in the story. Motion is a way to keep a quickening on the page. Status is a way to keep a quickening between the characters.

I introduce these strategies sequentially, but they're all part of a package. I ask my students to imagine that someone is walking past their play. That there are no seats. The audience is on its way to somewhere else. What stops them? What's the stop moment? It can be really simple.

A moment of beauty, a moment of people shouting at each other, someone playing a piccolo—it doesn't matter. What's the stop moment, and then—what's the stay moment? Two very different moments, and the stay moment is usually always going to be a question. What has happened? Why is this thing happening here? Who is that woman? We do not have the option of taking the audience's attention for granted. Attention is not passive, it is urgent. We must find mechanisms to keep what is happening on stage alive. The moving play is that thing that I'm watching, and it is shifting and changing and I have more and newer questions as I am watching it.

Maybe another writer can take for granted that the audience is just going to stay there and pay attention until it's over. I can't do that. We feed the audience to make them hungry.

I think a dangerous road that playwrights go down to make someone keep watching the scene is to make it really "interesting"—to make the characters busy doing really "interesting" things. I've failed when I've tried this. I think it's a zero-sum game. I think the more bells and whistles you use to entice attention, the further you get from the actual people that you're trying to write about. Instead, I'm looking for literal moments when a scene comes to life, moments which I call Turns: an escalation, major new information, a reversal, a surprise, a paradigm shift—all things that, when we're watching a scene, keep pulling us in. I try to put these tools in my playwrights' tool boxes—to root the energy of their scenes in the narrative turns rather than in the relationship or the meaning.

I'll do exercises where I'll give students some sort of rough rubric for a two- or three-character scene, something really simple—I'm trying to get them to make the scene purposeful, not "interesting." So those two or three pages are an exercise. It's not a little mini play they're writing. It's "playwright practice." It's going to the gym. There needs to be three Turns on every page. So there's a surprise or a reversal, and those can be enormous or tiny. These are exercises designed to make them see when a scene comes alive (and it is often easier to do this in an exercise than in the play they are working on). Okay, so: three turns on a page. Two status shifts in the scene. And sometimes I'll add a direct-address coda that has to be exactly three sentences long and include something that a character kept to himself during the scene. I do these kinds of exercises regularly in early semester classes until some of these mechanisms get explicitly, even shamelessly, learned.

What makes what I would call a turn? Imagine you're looking at a play like it's a globe, and something has turned … shifted … and now I'm looking at a different part of that globe. That play is now in a new moment, something has changed—I'm going to call that a turn. One example of a turn is escalation. Very simply:

1: I wanna cookie.
2: You wanna cookie?
1: *I WANNA COOKIE!!!*

Okay? That's escalation. It's a little bit like a turn on crack. You get a quick bit of lightning—and then it's over. But it can be useful in small doses, I think.

Surprise might be:

1. I wanna cookie.
2. They have arsenic in them.
1. I'll take four.

Reversal? How about:

1. I wanna cookie.
2. I'm keeping them.
1. I'm keeping this letter from your girlfriend.

Major New Info is not exposition—it's not having a character enter and say, "Wow, Starbucks was packed this morning." It is something that pushes the narrative forward with a leap, à la

1. Wanna cookie?
2. I'll get one in Phoenix. We're moving.

And just for fun, a Paradigm Shift might be:

1. I wanna cookie.
2. When you wake up, I'll give you one. You shouldn't eat in your dreams.

In each case, the play has turned slightly in the moment. And raised a new question. And kept living. These are all tangible ways to pump blood into a play and prompt change. Note that many of these strategies overlap with each other (a Reversal is likely always a Surprise, etc.), and I don't spend a minute of time trying to have students parse which is which. It doesn't matter. These are explicit tools that we practice in *purposefully artificial scenarios*, with often shameless results. But that flags them as tactics. And later they tend to arrive with greater and greater nuance in students' plays—both as generative tactics and revision ("My scene is dead, what do I do?") tactics.

This aspect of writing can be taught: making our skills and our craft more explicit and available to ourselves. To name and embrace the necessary machinery we seek to bundle to our (perhaps unteachable) improvisatory and renegade playwright mojo.

And of course there's always that point in the semester when I get the late-night e-mail: "Dietz, I'm trying to write my play, but all I'm thinking about is Turns! I'm thinking about Status! I'm thinking about the Time frame and function!"

And I say, "Excellent."

In anything you learn, the teaching is loud at first. And with mastery, the teaching grows quieter. Someone teaching you to ski—the teaching is so loud at first: "What do I do with my knees? The poles? Wait—I also have to breathe?!" There's a period where that's all the playwriting students can hear, and my job is to stay with them and get them to trust that the teaching gets quiet and they will—if they stick with it—inculcate the craft stuff that is useful.

I want them to learn to look at their own work rigorously. I want them to learn to invite (rather than wait for) scrutiny. I want to give them some of my operating language—they're stuck with my language for those fifteen weeks or three years or whatever—because my language in the classroom unifies them. Then they will need to get/make/find their own language. My job is to ultimately make myself unnecessary to them.

I want to write without inspiration. I want my students to be able to write without inspiration. I assume they will write when inspired—why wouldn't you? If they wake up and they're inspired every day and have a modicum of skill, they don't need anybody. They don't need me. But I don't believe we are inspired all the time. And we're working in a deadline art form. Craft, rigor, zest, grit, guile. If they graduate and think they can only write when they are inspired—when they "have a great idea for a play"—I will have failed them. I will have put them at the mercy of having a better idea than any playwright in America had that year. But if I can get them to not just work hard—that's too easy, to say that to students—but work *smart*, they will have careers. I want them to apply what they know and not just what they feel—maybe not right away, in early drafts, but over time, as they revise and reimagine. We do not become masters of our own work until we become students of our own work.

The idea for a play can be generated. The idea does not just have to be "found." I teach that you can actually find your way to the thing you didn't know you were going to write about. Plays don't land on us. Little bits of plays—a line, a gesture, a voice, a narrative move—that's what lands on us. What's the Oscar Wilde quote? "The first line of a poem falls from the ceiling. We cobble in the rest around it."

Young playwrights, all playwrights, walk around saying, "I need an idea for a play." You won't have one! A whole play will not land on you! You'll have an idea for a move, a scene, a moment, so *forgive yourself.* Forgive yourself that you're walking around saying, "I can't think of an idea for a play." You won't. You don't have to.

We also use it as an excuse: "Well … I'd love to be workin' today, but I don't really have any ideas for a play." That is a writer who is not serious. Pick a small thing. Make a move and go from there. The play has to be engineered. Your wild music will ultimately need some machinery. The play has to be made. *The play is the rigorous application of craft to the little idea that launched it.* The idea is often the smallest part of your play. We are not helped by the ongoing cultivation of this mythology: "If I have a great idea, I'll get a great play." My advice: have a small idea and work like mad. I suspect that's how you're going to get that great play.

We want writing made simple. It's not. It never will be. Here's as close as I can get to making it "simple": If I had a playwright emergency card that said, "Dietz, if something happens to you and you forget everything you know about playwriting, just read this card." The card would say: *Put the Idea/Image into Action, put the Action in Time.* So even if I don't have any inspiration, I will, as we talked about—have a rough idea or an image. Fatherhood. A chair. I can think up an idea or image. Even on the worst day. I don't have to have inspiration.

Let's say it's an image. You're going to put that in action, and then you're going to put that action in time. A necklace?—great. So if your image was that necklace, I'm going to encourage you to put that image in action. Suddenly, you'll have a character in your play. And that character's taking this necklace off and putting it in a small box. (And I'm going to remind you during the whole process not to make it interesting. Make it *purposeful.*) What is she doing? Why is that girl putting that necklace in that box? Here's where I encourage *Close Questioning.* Close questioning is the opposite of brainstorming. I think brainstorming is the death of collaboration and the demise of the American theater. Ha, you think I'm kidding. I'm not.

So you put the image in action: a young girl is putting the necklace back into a box. There's still nothing there, story-wise. *The moment it comes alive is when you place it in time. When* is this girl? *When* is this moment in her life? Not what era. When in her life? Her mother has passed away. Simple. Yes. Immediately I have a character. I have an event. I have a moment of *kairos*, a threshold moment for her. Notice how I already have two characters in the play, though only one has entered. Obviously I know her mother's in there. And somehow I know/suspect the necklace belonged to her mother. And now whatever the girl does with that necklace will give me something: if she refuses to wear it, if she sells it, if she saves it, if she remakes it. And story will follow, no matter which route I take. Image in action, action in time. Now circle around that woman, that necklace, her mother, and just explore that. Stay close. Think of the play as some vertical object, a tree or a pole or something; we can't just keep looking at our plays "this way"—from one direction. I want to encourage you to walk around your play. Maybe I walk around and realize the mother is telling this story. See where that goes. And we push on.

Don't make it interesting! I know you are trying to do that! You're going, "I'll think of an interesting thing." Don't! Make it simple! Let the idea be simple and the work be interesting. A boy is looking at a bookshelf! Okay, that's an image. I'll put this image into action. He's pulling one book out of a bookshelf. Now I apply the most important thing. I apply Time. Okay? *When* is this boy? This is much more important to my story-making than "who" is this boy. *Who* is speculative; *when* is actionable. When is this boy? When is it in this boy's life? Maybe he is packing to go to boarding school. I immediately have a story about a boy. He's going to take one book with him to boarding school. Again, this is the opposite of brainstorming, which I think of as the opposite of creative thinking. Brainstorming is typically "Just say the first thing that pops in your mind." Maybe it's not a book. Maybe it's a cookie jar! It's a cookie jar, and, no maybe it's a pound of radium and!—that's brainstorming.

I'm sure brainstorming has its value—like caffeine or karaoke—but our work is not to say the first thing that comes to our mind. Our work is to apply creative rigor to what we know already, in hopes of finding what we don't know yet. (Close questioning tries to stick the pins in the pincushion. This is harder and ultimately more purposeful than throwing the pins in the air.)

Our work is narrative energy in physical space, and what I want to suggest to you—and ask you to practice every day—is to learn to ask the close questions. I'm going to ask the closest questions around this boy. There's a bookshelf. A boy took a book down. Stay really close to that. What are my questions? What's the book? Why is he taking that book? Where is he going? Why is he going? Someone gave him that book. Is there an inscription? Something pressed inside? Has the book ever been read? By whom? If I know who gave him that book, I know why he's taking that book. I may or may not know why he's going… I will find that if I stay close in my questions. A boy is sent to boarding school. He can take one book. I've placed him in this moment in time. He thinks, *I have a huge bookshelf. I know the book I need. I take that book. I keep that book. I give that book away. I burn that book. I return that book to its owner.* It doesn't matter where we go from here. We're just story making, but we're staying close around that image, and most importantly, so far we haven't had any ideas! There's nothing here! Only our craft. You said a book, a bookshelf—we're building narrative. We're staying close, and the key thing is that we're making that moment central to him and purposeful and we're asking very, very close questions around him. This is so hard. I'll bet you're thinking, *Oh, this is so easy!* No. This is paying attention. Paying attention—over time—is very, very hard.

Writing takes rigor, and I do have a lot of exercises to build those muscles. I'll have my students write a scene, three pages max, keeping it really simple, where the setup is—two characters in an open space or two characters at a table. There's one object on the table. The scene is rooted in either a long overdue apology or a long overdue confrontation. I'm admittedly just charging the scene artificially so that it's not

    1: Good coffee, Joan.

    2: Thanks, Dietz.

When either character touches that object in any way, it is now either ten years later or ten years earlier. Suddenly we're making a story in Time, and that will force us into some moments of *kairos* for the characters. What's the big thing that happened ten years ago? What's the big thing that will happen ten years from now? So the students are just writing a scene. They're writing dialogue, but again, there's an artificial conceit here that makes them make a leap that may feel forced—and it is!—because I am trying to make their craft *explicit* to them. (And when I say artificial, think of pushups. We don't do the action of "pushing up" during our day, we recognize it as exercise and we do this odd thing to get stronger.)

To make matters harder (it is my job), I might bundle all that other stuff with a very simple status exercise, in which there's a third—unseen—character. I might assign that character's assumed status as very high for both of them, so immediately there's an offstage boss. Or that status is very low and immediately there's an offstage, I don't know, busboy. Then I might say: at the exact bottom of the third page, that third character enters and their status is revealed to be the exact opposite of what we (and perhaps the characters) thought. So they have a Status move, a Time move, Turns in the dialogue, etc. And this, friends, is hard as hell. Like a good workout.

I do all of these as discreet and individual exercises at first—but ultimately I pack all these things into one exercise. Why? Because then I am getting at some semblance of *all* that is going on in even the most simple scene. And the students will say, "I don't write this way! Dietz, this is not the way I write!" Which of course is true and also the perfect conversation starter because obviously I don't write that way either. But if they are serious—if they are signing on to learn some machinery to deliver their crazy music, to make their great cool unforgettably original ideas come to life, then this exercise has some tools for them. I would really feel like a fraud if I didn't give them tangible tools. I'm trying to teach to their fifth, seventh, ninth play. You get your first two or three plays for free. You write the play about your family, the play about your breakup, the play about the funny thing the guy told at the bar—you gotta write those plays. You get those first few plays for free! And God love 'em.

But then a few more plays into your career you realize, if you want to write *this* play—a play unlike any you've ever written before—you realize, "Oh shit. This requires stuff that I don't know how to do." This "stuff" isn't handed to you in my exercises, but—like so many things—the practice expands the thinking. It teaches the students to walk around their ideas, their plays, and apply strategies from differing angles. Most of these writing tools are intuitive things that I've simply given names to.

I am deeply invested in active language. So I ask playwrights to look out for what I call dialogue traps. Why? Because if you keep looking at a scene of dialogue on page seventeen, and rereading page seventeen, and page seventeen is just flat and dull and lifeless … I'll bet it's not that you need a "great new idea." I'll bet one of four language traps is happening on that page.

The traps I point to are: answered questions; stated emotions; transitional phrases; and double sentences. Now, of course there can be answered questions and stated emotions and transitional phrases and double sentences in your play—but eventually these things, alone or in tandem, will spell the end of any motion in your scene. I give these to students as tangible things (I believe we owe our students tangible things) to look for when their dialogue just feels like chat. Does the American theater need more chat? I don't think so.

Answered questions produce a ping-pong effect:

1:   Do you wanna go to the store?
2:   Yes:
1:   What time should we leave?
2:   Nine.
1:   I'll meet you at my house?
2:   That's great.
1:   You wanna go to a movie later?
2:   Yes.

This is a good dialogue trap. It just makes things flat. Instead, you can answer a question with a question. You can jump the answer. Anything but more ping-pong.

Another trap: Stated Emotions.

1.   I am so angry at you, Angela.
2.   Well, Bill, I used to love you. I don't anymore.

Embody, rather than name, the emotion. You'll be surprised how alive the exchange may become.

Another trap: Transitional Phrases. That's a great way to kill language. Phrases like "You know what I mean" or "anyway" or "Sure, okay, but—" Imagine if Williams wrote, "Well, still and all, I have always depended on the kindness of strangers, you know?" It would still sound pretty beautiful. The "d" would still have a nice bite against the "k" and the run of "s's" would still produce ache. But it wouldn't be nearly as memorable. Why? An active sentence has been made passive by its transitions (that were likely inserted to make it sound like "how people really talk").

Double Sentences. This is the ultimate one. If I could take your play and rid it of double sentences, your play would almost surely come to life. Double sentences:

1. Anyone want to go to Bell's? I like that place.
2. Yeah, it's good. I've been there a lot.
3. Let's call Tony. He's a good time.
4. That guy can party. He can go all night.

Every one of those speeches is a double sentence and will prove completely lulling over time. Again, the point is not "people really talk like that" or "that's how I hear this character" or "what's the big deal, it's just a few words," the point is the aural and narrative impact, over time, of these traps.

Plays live and die in small moments, in the energy and efficacy of small exchanges. This beat does not have much to achieve (other than chat), so if I remove the double sentences, I might get:

1. Anyone want to go to Bell's?
2. Call Tony. He can go all night.

I'll now write you a scene. It's a masterpiece, I'm certain. It is one page long. I'd encourage you to consider the dialogue traps we have talked about as you listen to my very good scene. It's called "The Hallway."

Vic and Lila wait at the end of a darkened hallway.

Vic: Okay, no matter what you say now, before you said you'd go down there with me. You said that. I heard you.

Lila: I know I said that, Vic, but that was before we said goodbye to those two people who never came back after they went down there. I'm not so sure I want to do that now anyway.

Vic: Lila, please, how bad can it be? I have a candle, and I have a whistle, and I can probably, I don't know, borrow, like, a knife or something, you know?

Lila: The reason that I came here is that I really wanted to ask you something. Something I've always really wondered about.

Vic: Go ahead and ask me then.

Lila: Well this is it: How did you get over losing her? I never have. None of us ever have. None of us, but you, Vic. You've done it.

Vic: The way I did it was to become someone else. It's easy. I'm not me anymore. I'm a fearless man who will walk with you down this hallway til its end, and no matter what happens, I'll be okay with it. See?

Lila: You mean to say you don't ever think of her?

Vic: I'm not saying that. I'm thinking of her right now. I think of her whenever I look at you. Every single time.

Lila: What do you mean by that? I don't understand.

Vic: She was afraid of the hallway too. Just like you are. You're the same that way, but she walked down it anyway, and it was the last thing she ever did, Lila.

"The Hallway"—a masterpiece by Steven John Dietz. (Why are you laughing?) Now I will go through it and remove only the following traps: answered questions, stated emotions, transitional phrases, double sentences. Here's what I get:

Vic: You said you'd go down there with me.

Lila: Those two people never came back.

Vic: I have a candle, a whistle. I can borrow a knife.

Lila: You don't ever think of her?

Vic: I'm thinking of her right now.

Okay, there's no masterpiece in here, but that revision required no thinking, no ideas. It required me making a list of ideas that were just chat, that were just typing, that were just my fingers doing a scene. And the other thing is, if I have a ninety-page play and then I just get up and do my work on these traps (which always embed themselves in early drafts, no shame in that), now I have a forty-five-page play. This is fantastic. I now have an extra forty-five pages for my story. The notion that I put all that other stuff in just to generate pages will never be helpful to me in the long run.

Writing like people talk is not enough. As Ben Marcus beautifully observed, "The sentence as a technology is used for so many rote exchanges, so many basic communicative requirements that to rescue it from these unnecessary mundanities, to turn it into feeling, is to do something strenuous and heroic."

Write with power. Write with boldness. Write with vivid magic. Grant your characters that great strong language that fails you or me in our day-to-day life. I do an exercise where we try to make good sentences bad as a way of showing that the unforgettable sentence is always embedded in the average, daily sentence. An example: "Everywhere you look, someone's acting." What's that? "All the world's a stage, and all the men and women merely players."

What about "People I don't know have always helped me out." In the right hands, that sentence becomes, of course, "I've always depended on the kindness of strangers." Or maybe "He worked for the phone company." Nothing wrong with that. Until you hear: "He was a telephone man who fell in love with long distance."

Great writing has great motion. That is the crucial element—whether delivered by character or language or event. The questions (small and big) that the audience is asking need to continue to change. It's a great exercise to write at the top of every page what the question on that single page is. And I don't mean theme. Do not descend into theme. There's no help for you when you descend into theme. When you descend into theme you can say, "Well, the question is really about whether love can conquer the trappings of a difficult family." That's fantastic. I can't direct that. I can't act that. You can't revise that because there is nothing tangibly there.

What's the real and present question on the page (and don't sweat if it is simple)? When will Brenda arrive? Great question. Doesn't have to be artful. Turn the page, page two: What's the question? When will Brenda arrive? When will Brenda arrive? If I have the same question at the top of the page for, I don't know, fifteen to twenty pages, what's wrong? Perhaps everything! Unless the energy system of the play is built around the arrival of Brenda, the play isn't moving. And even if it is, we are hungry for other more present and proximate questions as we wait. And I don't mean there is not stuff happening (see earlier discussion of action!), I mean nothing is changing. If I have the same question at the top of page after page after page, I know there hasn't been a shift. There hasn't been a turn. There has been no narrative motion.

One exercise I do with my students is to make them write a full-length play in thirty pages. And they often say, "You mean a short play."

I say, "No, I do not. I mean a full-length play in thirty pages."

"Well I can't do that."

And I say, "Really? How much actual play do you think is in your full-length play? In that ninety-page play you have, how much actual motion do you think is in there? On how many of those ninety pages is something or someone changing? How many pages have a quickening? A shift? A new and deepening question? Bring me only those pages."

And usually I just get a handful of pages from those students. The other pages typically have the setup—this lets you know that they're in Biloxi, Mississippi, in 1973 and that their grandpa, etc.— and these pages have them chatting about stuff that happened before or might happen someday, the pages in which we "get to know" the characters. There are a *lot* of those pages. But typically, let's say, only about fifteen of the ninety have narrative motion—what I sometimes call the "is," the thing, the real part. The part that is alive and quickening in Time. That is the gold.

To actively question and scrutinize our own play is much harder than the writing, and it won't get better unless you do that. I don't mean "take notes from people." Of course do that, if the notes are helpful to you. *But most of your notes should come from you. And there should be a lot of them, and they should be rigorous and potent and actionable.*

Read plays. Study how the author is using time to make the narrative come to life. Find the triggering event, the central question, and how the questions we are asking as the audience keeps changing and deepening. Underline the unforgettable sentences. See where the short word is. Note how actively the sentence is crafted. Steal the good verbs.

I think we've established a weird little world in which utterly fantastic students will say to me, "Well, I really want to rewrite it, Dietz—but I'll do rewrites after I get people's notes." I used to just let them say that, because of course on some level it makes sense, but … I now know that that is insufficient. It is an abdication. Of course invite scrutiny and make great use of it—but rewriting only when you get feedback is problematic. It's on you. Do your work.

To the playwright who doesn't have a built-in writing community, I would say, "If you can take a workshop, if you can take a class, if you can find a way to hear the play, tell the story of that scene to a friend. Tell the story of that character to a friend. Practice the world of the play over and over again. If you have two or three characters in the play, tell me the story of the play in the first person—never use the word 'they'—tell it from 'I' with each character, from all their points of view. See what you learn. I think you will learn where your story is alive and where it has gaps."

Ultimately, when you as a playwright can read your work aggressively—hear your work openly—and revise your work fearlessly, then, I think, you find your voice and your story.

There are a few things that I think every playwright must have: audacity; empathy; craft; guile; grit; patience. But if you want to continue to hone your craft as a playwright, you also have to find your mentors and find your group—finding that group of playwrights to hear your plays. And I'll just add that if you're the best playwright in your group, you're in the wrong group. Play in the bracket above you. Be pals with everybody and find your support network, but be in the room with playwrights you envy. Self-produce on a small scale. Don't write your masterpiece. Write the play in front of you. Make a great collaborator, which is different from finding a great collaborator, and make someone your collaborator. Build them and let them build you.

Sharpen yourself against the playwrights who don't write the plays like you do. Find a director or a dramaturg you love. Put them in your pocket, and then make sure you work with a wildcard person every now and then who will be your nudge, your nemesis, your irrational provocateur. And then the silly thing is: just write. You may laugh at that, but I have a good buddy who, when we all started playwriting together, wrote the best play of any of us, by far. And that play had thirty-seven staged readings, and then he finally self-produced it in the '90s. And during those probably seventeen years, he never wrote anything else.

Write the play in front of you. Keep doing it. It sounds so simple. Do that daily work. Whatever your daily practice is. Make sure you have a daily practice. That same good buddy—who is now a drummer, shaman, and healer—reminds me that any great practice requires great faith, great doubt, and great commitment. When you get up in the morning, the play's just waiting for you. Your play doesn't leave. Your play never gives up on you. Have you ever woken up and gone to your desk and your play is gone? No! Believe me. Your play wakes up and sits around all sorts of days and *you're* gone. "She hasn't come back! Where the hell did my playwright go?!"

So let's talk about what we control and what we don't. We don't control the new play market. We don't control the decisions of artistic leaders or critics or audiences. We don't control very many things at all, but we can do our work. We have twenty-six letters and thousands of days. There's nothing between us and the language. There are all sort of things between us and a career. But there's nothing standing between us and our work. That's maddening, I know. Maddening in the best possible way.

BETH HENLEY

I teach an undergraduate playwriting course at Loyola Marymount University in Los Angeles. The class is open to students across campus and there are no prerequisites. I get theater majors, screenwriting majors, English majors, as well as those studying mechanical engineering, biology, international studies, and so forth, signing up. The challenge is to make this class of twelve random students weave into a small theater company.

As the class is only one semester, I don't have time to go into "advanced" anything. All is with the beginner's mind. My secret hope and desire is that students leave the class bewitched by theatre.

To write plays, one must see plays, read plays, act in plays, and study playwriting. My students spend the semester learning to do these things. Then their final project is to write a ten-minute play as well as a monologue that is either in their play or enlightens it. The monologue does not necessarily have to be a part of the play. It can be used as a way to discover more about a character that is in the play.

I want students to write from a place of love. Singular and personal love. A remarkable quote from Eudora Welty helps explain this thought:

> And so finally I think we need to write with love. Not in
> self-defense, not in hate, not in the mood of instruction,
> not in rebuttal, in any kind of militancy, or in apology,
> but with love. Not in exorcisement, either, for this is to
> make the reader bear a thing for you.

Neither do I speak of writing forgivingly; out of love you can write with straight fury. It is the source of the understanding that I speak of; it's this that determines its nature and its reach. How does a writer discover the source of love within herself? There is no answer. Exploration and striving are part of it. It helps to find life's paradoxes fascinating. Chekhov tells us to write without judgment or agenda. He says, "To a chemist nothing on earth is unclean."

On the first day of class I read another famous quote—this one from Martha Graham—that urges students to embrace a personal creative state: "There is a vitality, a life force, an energy, a quickening that is translated through you into action, and because there is only one of you in all of time, this expression is unique."

So within the class, I encourage students to discover who they are as artists, to find their singular expression. Another thing I emphasize is listening. Listen closely and consistently.

Early in the class I hand out a questionnaire to the students that asks for the following.

Your Name
A favorite:
Play
Playwright
Holiday
Animal
Toy you remember (describe it):
Do you have a scar? Explain.
What are you afraid of?
What is your dream?
What makes you laugh?
Can love die?
What do you want to learn from this class?

When they finish the quiz, I take my book bag and have everyone write their name on a piece of paper and drop it in. This is fun in a subversive way because I don't indicate it's anything other than a functional action—dropping one's name into a bag.

I draw two names randomly. Making it random helps take the pressure off of the students and off of me. No one is chosen or not chosen. Fate decides. The two students who are chosen sit before the class. One student interviews the other and then they reverse roles. The interviewer may ask one question from the quiz. This helps start things easily, as the student being interviewed has already answered the question. Listening deeply, the interviewer must ask five follow-up questions to that one question. How much can one discover by asking questions and, more importantly, *listening*?

The exercise encourages curiosity, listening, and telling. There is an art to listening as well as telling. Certain courage is involved.

One of the things I tell my students is: When all else fails and there is nothing left—*don't forget courage.*

Another motto I stress: SHOW UP. Woody Allen says that showing up is 80 percent of what one needs to be a success. For me, showing up means not only coming to class but also being present and engaged. It's important to be there for the whole company. Some students may be having a play read for the first time in their lives. I usually have the class sit in a circle so the connection becomes literal.

Wondering what can be taught in playwriting? Imagination, observation, and experience (Faulkner's big three) can be encouraged and enhanced. This is what I emphasize in my class. What one cannot teach is, to quote Walker Percy, "a little knack for writing. Or perhaps it is desire, a kind of underhanded desire."

This is in the realm of gifts. I can't know if a student is gifted in one semester. Thus, I make the assumption that all my students have gifts they can discover, gifts that might widen their vision of being alive.

In the second class, I explore what it takes to begin to write. Beginning is hard. I do a lecture on beginnings—how difficult it is, because it's just a white piece of paper. I compare that to a chapter in *Moby Dick* that is all about the terror of the white whale, and what a primitive terror whiteness can be. I talk about allowing time, space, and boredom. Diane Arbus notes: "The Chinese have a theory that you pass through boredom into fascination." I think it's true.

I also like to put forth the idea of confusion. When I first thought of writing, I believed being wise, informed, and talented were minimum criteria for putting words onto paper. However, I came upon an article interviewing Ionesco, where he said, "I write out of my confusion."

For me this was profound. I reasoned, I am permanently and always confused. I excelled in confusion. I will write out of my own confusion. I discovered that true confusion is dramatic and compelling. In drama, it is better not to know the story you are writing. It should evolve out of the pain and search of confusion.

After telling the class to be confused, I confuse them more by handing out five mini plays from *L-Play,* a brave failure I wrote in the nineties. I somewhat randomly assign students parts in the plays. They read over the play that they have been cast in, and then I talk to the whole class about each play. I discuss the theme, style, and story. Each play has a different theatrical style, which lets them see that a play doesn't have to be people talking in a kitchen. It opens up some possibilities.

In the third class they are performing, script in hand, staged versions of the playlets. They must understand that plays are written to be performed—in real time and real space, before an audience. I want the class to experience the lift a story takes when it is given the dignity of being staged and spoken while it is seen and heard. This gives them a glimmer of the process as well as a chance to work with each other.

By the fourth class we're doing in-class writing exercises. One of my favorites deals with developing imagination:

- Imagine an isolated outdoor space.
- What time of day is it?
- What kind of weather?
- How does the sky look?
- Imagine a tree you've never seen in real life. Describe the tree: size, color, bark, roots, leaves, old or young?
- Imagine a terrible wind blows the tree. After the wind subsides, write a brief monologue for the tree describing the event.
- Ask the tree its name. Write answer.
- Ask the tree what it wants to tell you. Write answer.
- Imagine you have a strong sharp axe.
- Ask the tree what it would like you to do with the axe. Write answer.
- Tell the tree you're going to do the opposite of what it wants you to do.
- Explain to the tree why you have to do this.
- Write.

This exercise gives students experience creating dialogue and writing a monologue. They flex their imagination, creating an otherworldly tree and giving it language. Story-wise, a plot is developed. Will the tree be axed? The character of Tree is developed. Tree has a name, knowledge, experience, and a desire.

An exercise given to me by a former student, the writer Brian Shuff, is called "Worst Play Ever Written." The students must write a scene from the worst play ever written, after which they write a review of the play written by a bitter alcoholic critic. These scenes are often more original and provocative than plays the students spend the semester working on. I think it is because the challenge is to write horribly and fail miserably. And that's fun. That is play.

The next step is for the students to begin writing their ten-minute play. To help, I give them "Assignment Solo:"

- They must find a space where they will not be interrupted.
- They must turn off all electronics.
- They must do this for a clearly timed four hours. Doing it in two sessions is allowed.
- I suggest using a timer that goes off every twenty-three minutes.
- If they are interrupted or use electronics, they must make a note explaining how this happened and find a solution that will keep it from happening again.
- They must give this space to their play.
- Plays need time and space. Characters demand it. And developing this practice is important. In the following class, students talk about their solo experience in detail. They give each other tips and strategies.

It's important for my students to understand that the act of writing itself has value. It doesn't matter what you write, just that you write. Discoveries will be made, ideas will come. There will be times when you're not inspired to write. The theory of writer's block is just part of the process. You show up. You write a string of obscenities for two hours. Or draw a picture of a dog. Make your grocery list. I've discovered that once you put pen to paper or fingers to keys, it is likely that something will be written. When something has been written, it can be accepted or rejected. If accepted, one has a glimmer of insight. If rejected, one can become aware of why it is wrong and what might be right. The writer is into action/reaction, which is a dynamic creative place.

The students present a first draft of their ten-minute play in class. They present a monologue. After the first reading of the play, I ask the playwright, "What did you think?" I listen and then ask many questions. It slowly becomes clear what is and is not coming across as intended. Often the playwrights have no idea what they intended. The exploration of what has been written helps them discover paths the play might be inclined to take. I encourage them to look carefully at their work—to deal with specifics. Do I need this sentence? Why isn't this clear? Do I like this character's hat? I also ask the class for feedback, but to me the most important thing is to teach writers how to mine the gold in the dregs of an early draft.

They rewrite and then present a revised version of their play and monologue. I have them bring in scripts for each character, a script for stage directions, and a script for the professor. The plays are staged and performed by students in the class. The writers can see what has improved and what needs further thought and revision.

I encourage them to continue to develop their plays after the class concludes. I hope that they come to understand that commitment to the development of the work is key to its success; two drafts is only a beginning.

Because going to the theater is new to some of my students, I ask them to see three plays and tell the class about the experience. There is no paper or criticism required. I want them to go to a theater, buy a ticket, sit in an audience, watch a play, and applaud it. The theater is for play. And talking about that experience allows them—and sometimes me—to begin to consider the entirety of the art form.

Recently, a student of mine who does not major in theater went to see her first play. I asked her what it was like. She said, "Dark." This intrigued me because the play she had gone to see was the musical *Nine.*

"Dark?" I asked. "You found the play dark?"

"No, not the play," she said, "the theater. It got so dark before it began."

I realized she meant the *lights* go dark. It made me rethink the power of that light-to-dark-to-light moment in theatre. Before the play begins, there is a moment when strangers sit together in the dark, waiting to watch a story. Waiting to suspend disbelief and to be together in the light of imagination.

We discuss theatrical elements, finding examples in their plays. The students look at images, tone, style, theme, and setting. We explore characters: their age, education, and culture; their wants, their desires. In drama, characters need to desire something, because if you don't desire something, there is no conflict. Desire plus conflict equals action or inaction—and that equals drama. What also must be discovered is the struggle a character has within his soul. Faulkner speaks of "the problem of the human heart in conflict with itself." What does the character fear most and desire most? Macbeth would not be interesting if he had no fear, if he had no conscience, if he wasn't torn, or if he was just a villain.

It's a subtle thing for people to understand. But it's very important. Blanche, from Williams's *A Streetcar Named Desire*, wants to be pure white, a saint on a pedestal, and yet she has sexual longings, fears, demons, and rage. These conflicting feelings are what bring her to the action of the play.

I think that investing in the deep study of a play, looking at all its elements and all its demands, broadens students' ability to think about writing. So I'll have them read a play three times. The first time, they are simply to read it through—to get a sense of the play; the second time, they must go very slowly and look up any words or references that are unfamiliar, and make certain they know the linear movement of the play if it is out of sequence. I ask them: What did you grasp after reading the play the second time that you had not realized? I want them to look carefully at these discoveries, the subtleties of the writing. The last time they read the play straight through. I ask what changed for them from the first reading to the last.

I also ask them to take the play apart. They must: explain how their views on the play changed, evolved after each reading; give a summary of the story of the play; describe the main characters; discuss the use of time and place in the play; describe the opening and closing moments of the play; discuss theatrical moments presented in the play; and choose a section of the play to be read in class (three to six pages) that illustrates the drama of the play.

By reading the play three times, the students become familiar with the characters, story, structure, and tone. They begin to become aware of how information is parsed out. How and when plot and character are revealed is key to dramatic storytelling. By reading a play three times, one begins to see the playwright's craft.

Coming to teaching has been hard for me. I'm not a natural guider. More than anyone, actors have been my teachers. They memorize lines I have written and bring life to characters I have faintly imagined. Their performances extend my comprehension of elements in the play. They reveal things I would not have imagined.

It has taken me years to know how to show up for my own class. The trick is caring. You have to care a lot.

Finally, new playwrights need to understand that they own the copyright to their play. Any changes they make in a workshop or production need to enhance their vision of the play and must also belong to them. Professional advice I would give to young playwrights: join the Dramatists Guild.

Lucas Hnath

I think my greatest strength as a playwriting teacher lies in the area of developing or rewriting a play. What I've become most interested in is a model of teaching that is about the students identifying what they value and then giving them the tools to assess whether or not their play is matching those values, and if not, what they can do to make the play they want to write.

Lately, I've become kind of disenfranchised with what I would call the "oracle" model of teaching, which is not to say that it's a bad thing at all, but I have noticed a lot of playwriting workshops fall into the pattern of having students bring in ten pages of a play in progress, and after hearing feedback from fellow students, the teacher delivers some "expert advice." I think these days I'm reacting against that and as much as possible trying to remove myself from the position of the person that you're coming to for approval or to tell you if what you're doing is right or wrong.

I think the first time that I started practically exploring the idea was when I moved into teaching in the universities and I had to contend with the problem of grades. How do you grade playwriting? Which is a really interesting practical problem to me. Either you just sort of refuse and you just say, "Well, you just show up and do the work and you get an A," but then that sort of makes the act of grading no longer an evaluation tool.

I was thinking a lot about first drafts of plays—and how do you evaluate a first draft? Some people crank out a first draft, and it's really tight, and some people crank out a really messy one. Both are valuable, so I decided to not grade or evaluate their first drafts. The final piece that they submit for the semester is an evaluation of their play, where they talk about what in their play works and why, what they think doesn't work and why they think it doesn't work, what they're planning to do in the next draft to take on the stuff that they don't think works as well as they would like, and why they think those strategies would be useful. What I end up grading isn't their play but rather their thinking about their play. I'm not grading whether I think they are right or wrong. I'm grading the rigor and coherence and specificity of thought.

Part of the challenge in taking stock of their plays is that I think that too few playwrights have sufficient language to talk about how plays work; they struggle with talking about plays—others and their own. To phrase that a little differently, I think we have very little language to talk about style in plays. In visual art, there seems to be a lot more, at the very least, jargon—that's a starting place. So I ask my students to read other texts and in some way account for how they work, and I use several methods to get them there.

I do find that drawing how it works is really useful, and I think that's a method that a number of other playwriting teachers use. They use maps. This is even a little influenced by Suzan-Lori Parks's introduction to *The America Play and Other Works*. She has some maps in there. My students get frustrated initially because I won't really give parameters or a structure. I just say read a scene and draw a picture that in some way helps me understand how that scene works. Which raises a whole other question. What do I mean by "work"? What does it mean for something to work? They'll draw something, but the important part is when I say, "Okay, show us the drawing and explain to us how the drawing shows us something useful about how the play works." It's in translating the drawing into language that they start to come up with language that helps account for how the play works.

There's even simpler groundwork that I do. There's this scene from Caryl Churchill's *Mad Forest* between a dog and a vampire. Those characters don't show up before the scene or after the scene. It's a wonderful scene because it's about four pages long, and it does in fact have a beginning, middle, and end. It's completely self-contained. I often do this exercise on the first day of class to get us developing language, and get the students articulating something about the play. I'll say to read it twice and then make the simplest change to the scene that would break it. Then present that change and explain how that actually breaks the scene—turns it from a scene that works into one that's not working. Sometimes the question "Why does this work?" freezes people up, but there's some perverse fun about breaking a scene and making it worse as a pathway for talking about what does it mean for something to work.

I find that pretty reliably they'll get to answers with less BS in them. I love even having students just write out an explanation and look at the language they use. There's all these placeholder words that stand in for something more meaningful. I think one of the most common is "connect." What are the characters doing in the scene? Well, they're trying to "connect." That means a lot of things, and the fact that you're using that word means that something very potent is happening, but "connect" often alludes to some kind of transaction or exchange. If you can name what's being exchanged, then you can explore what it is about that scene that is effective, why it draws us in and makes us want to watch.

Playwriting trouble often comes from misidentifying how a play works. A really common example is what happens when my students read Annie Baker's plays. You ask them, "So what do you appreciate about the play?"

They say, "Well, nothing happens in the play, and that's what I like about it."

What do you mean by "nothing happens"? There's a sense in which that label makes sense, and there's a sense in which it's wildly inaccurate. If students can identify what the characters are doing in her plays and why that's compelling, then they start to have a clearer idea of how the writer achieves the effects she achieves. I think that a lot of playwriting trouble comes from the language we use to talk back to ourselves about plays being too vague.

For example, if you show students five scenes from five different plays, and you ask them to describe the style of those five plays, oftentimes the language they use will be words like "realistic, surreal, absurd;" maybe they'll say "naturalistic," but it stops there. These could be scenes that are wildly different in terms of style, but they're going to flatten the difference if they don't have the language to talk about it.

I started this exercise two semesters ago. I say, "The subject of this artwork is the crucifixion," and I bring in five depictions of the crucifixion from over the course of the history of art. They're all completely different. I start with Hieronymus Bosch's *Crucifixion with a Donor* and end on Francis Bacon's *Three Figures at the Base of the Crucifixion*. We spend some time just developing language for how to talk about style, coining language to talk about these images.

Then I say, "Now let's move from images to plays, and the subject of all of these plays will be "domestic life." We look at five excerpts and images from plays in domestic settings, and I ask them to match those with the works of art in terms of style. Which is the Francis Bacon living room? Edward Albee's *Who's Afraid of Virginia Woolf*? That starts to take us in the direction of the world of Francis Bacon. Finding visual language to talk about style seems to be productive.

The work I do with students often has something to do with looking at a work that's not your own, poking around, learning something, and transferring that same frame of thinking back to your own work. In any class where I'm attempting to rigorously teach rewriting, I'll give them two different drafts of one of my plays, and I'll ask them to write down everything that changed from one draft to the next, and then rank what they think are the five most important changes I made and why, to try to explain back to me my thinking. What that yields in class is a kind of broader discussion about the kinds of changes that make the biggest differences. They list those and then see if they can apply those kinds of adjustments back to their own plays. But I also want them to use the discussion as a springboard for deciding what kind of dramaturgy is most relevant to what they're making, and maybe the kinds of changes I made to my play don't apply to their plays. And if not, then they need to explain why and identify what it is that their play needs.

Another thing that I've been thinking about applies to rewriting but doesn't exclusively apply to it, although again I find it most useful in that phase when you just have a messy draft of something. I've been really interested in the subject of wants or objectives. I've been interested in it because I have found that it seems a little taboo in playwriting pedagogy. A lot of writers teach steer away from it, and I understand why because when you ask a student, "So what does your character want?" They tend to freeze. They look like a deer caught in headlights. There's a little bit of panic and, if they do say something, they oftentimes grab onto a want or objective that is kind of flat, that has a kind of generic quality to it. Or they'll just tell me what a character *doesn't* want. I have all sorts of theories about why we get so weird when asked about wants or objectives. But what I've been asking myself is, what do we have the easiest time identifying? If naming objectives is hard, and in the worst-case scenario stifles creativity, what are students more willing to talk about? What stokes creativity?

What I've noticed is that we often enjoy talking about problems. There's a perverse kind of fun in enumerating all the troubles a particular character has in life, and so I've thought a lot about indulging that impulse in the writing process. I'll have students look at a text we're studying in class and just list all the problems the characters have in the play. That quickly fills one column. Then you can have a second column next to that and have a little arrow drawn off from each problem: "and so what?" The character encounters this problem, and so they do what? Then you list the actions the character takes in the play as a result of each problem.

The movement between problem and action is really easy to find in a very wide range of different plays from different traditions. It's really easy to break down a play into a chain of problems and actions. Then I find that once they see this in a play that they didn't write, students have an easier time seeing the possible relationship between problem and action in their own play. They see this problem and this problem and this problem and this problem, and you can push them a little further and say, okay, "Explain why those problems are problems, just flesh it out." Then you can say, "For each of those problems, what actions follow?" So they brainstorm actions. What's interesting is, if you look at the relationship between characters' problems and actions they take, somewhere in between there is an implicit want, but it's almost like this back-door entry into "objective" that's motivated by danger, motivated by problems, motivated by pain.

For the most part, their characters do very little in early drafts. This isn't true with every student, but I would say there is a trend where there's a great deal of angst, or a hint of pain, or trouble, but the early drafts seem to mostly be about identifying or starting to explore characters' problems or what they're unhappy about. Again, it's just a trend, but it often seems to be the case that toward the end of a draft, a character might do something, and then the play's over. But I think that's because, in part, they tend to have a limited definition of action. First and foremost they'll think that action means physical action. It's almost as if that word suggests something like action film, like a physical fight. So the work of simply identifying in another play the range of what constitutes action is really useful because it is actually a verb problem. They have limited verbs in mind when they go to work. I've noticed that expanding vocabulary opens up possibilities for their own plays that they're just not thinking of.

I try not to, but I really do end up using a lot of the same plays, over and over with some variation. I especially love teaching Fornes's *Mud*. If you graph that play according to problem and action, it is like a latticework, just beautifully constructed. It's so tight. Fornes is brilliant at writing relatively short scenes that make a huge difference. You're in a completely different place by the end of those two pages.

There are other plays that I teach because I find that their study also explores the idea of action in important ways. I teach Laura Marks's *Bethany* for similar reasons that I teach *Mud*. The movement between problems and actions is really tight in that play. There's very little fat in it. It ends up becoming something you can use to very quickly get them to see the shape of a play. Caryl Churchill's *A Number* expands their language around action because they'll often be very quick to say that the father, Salter, doesn't do anything in the play, which is demonstrably not true. His character opens up the possibility that, oh yeah, lying—that's an action. You can also demonstrate there's actually something he's trying to get out of his sons. It's really as simple as him trying to get them to tell him he's a good father. It can be that simple.

We read Edward Albee's *The Goat*, and I ask students to reduce the play down to thirty lines of dialogue and twelve stage directions. The objective is to reduce the play in such a way that you can read through those lines and those stage directions and actually get the story. It's very difficult because often what they'll do is include their favorite lines, but those aren't necessarily the lines that tell the story. You can actually tell that story in thirty lines of dialogue if you pick the lines that are decisions or lines that change another character's decision. I also like doing that exercise because there really are at least twelve very important stage directions. I'll ask them, "Do you have at least twelve really important stage directions in your play?" Which is to say, you don't have to, but are you using that tool? Because you have it available. You could use it.

I have found that by asking students to do this exercise with their own plays, they can get a bird's eye view of their play, and that can be extremely helpful. I might ask them to do this at two different points in the writing process. They might do it at an early stage of writing. So let's say they've been working on a play idea for a few weeks, I'll say, "Okay, just race ahead. Try to write out the whole play in thirty lines." That's really hard. I've done it myself, and it can be overwhelming early on. But sometimes the exercise is helpful at an early stage because it is a way of getting them to outline, but in a more intuitive way. It's an outline that's not an outline. It's an outline that's in the characters' voices. And in indirectly outlining their plays, they might divine an important moment that they want to work toward as they continue building their first draft.

And then I'll have them do the exercise later, when they are rewriting. I ask them to reduce the play so that they become conscious of their play's most essential elements.

For a long time I thought about how do you teach voice? How do you teach language? How do you teach dialogue? I like teaching it at a point in the semester when they've read a bit of Churchill, they've read a bit of Fornes, and they've done a good bit of writing. Maybe they've written a few different pieces, little bits and stuff. I'll spend some time getting them to describe how Fornes and Churchill use language. How would you describe a style of dialogue in those plays? I invite them to come up with their own invented terms. I'll ask them to come up with a title to describe the style that includes a noun and an adjective, and it can very be impressionistic. One student described Churchill's voice as "surgical empathy," and another described Fornes as "jagged heartbreak." Then, in explaining their titles, they actually start to articulate how Churchill characters tend to talk and how Fornes characters tend to talk, and then I'll have them look for trends in their own work. I'll say, take out the last three exercises that you did. How would you describe how you tend to use language? Then we read Anne Carson's *Grief Lessons* and translations of four different Euripides plays. Particularly, I like teaching *Alcestis*.

At the end of the play, Alcestis is rescued from death, having been horribly wronged by her husband. But Euripides doesn't allow her to talk at the end of the play. So we look at that last scene, we talk about the characters, and then I'll say, "I'm going to make one revision to the play. I want you to imagine she can talk—so what does she have to say to her husband?"

Then they write these monologues that just kind of let loose. I mean, they are just incredibly brutal and honest and really specific. Then I'll say, now write it as Anne Carson would write it, in her voice. Then write it in the voice of Fornes. Then write it in the voice of Churchill. Then, lastly I say now write it in your own voice. That act of writing in a style of another writer has been really useful in terms of getting them to start recognizing what their own voice might be in a way that, hopefully, isn't too self-conscious but helps them zero in on something they tend to like to do.

Everything I've talked about so far has probably not come out of my writing as much as it's come out of teaching and then come back to my writing. But there's one exercise that I took from Simon Stephens that I think he took from David Lan. He has his students each think of a play that they really love and then describe that play in five events. What are the five events that happen in this play that are most important to this play? Write them in order. Then you pair up with another student—all the students have picked different plays—and you try to figure out a kind of outline that accounts for both of your plays. So you have two different students with two different plays and two different sets of five events. Can you come up with a five-step outline that describes both plays accurately? And they do so. Then everybody comes together and tries to mash together their five-step outlines. It always turns out a little bit differently, but you end up with this über outline for plays that to some degree is kind of expected but will often have sort of surprising insight about a certain thing that tends to happen in plays.

For a while I would do this exercise with students, and I would take that outline and use it to help me write my next play. Of course the truth is you depart from it, you break it. I would tell them that what you come up with, that's going be my next play, and it sort of raises the stakes in a way that is fun for all of us. They're not at stake—I am at stake. I really did do that for a while. Every time I do that exercise, I learn something like, oh yeah, a lot of plays tend to do this one thing. The last time we did it, I think we discovered that in all our plays, whatever the central character seemed to be trying to do, the students all kind of realized around point four that he was going about it in the wrong way. That's a typical sort of narrative convention, but there's something in the way the students described it that that gave me a new thought about how to do that on stage that absolutely affected my writing.

That's the way I approach teaching. I always put at stake whatever play I'm writing at the time. I never have a single, fixed lesson plan. I rigorously design my courses, but every semester it's different. In part, it's about me having a play that I'm trying to figure out how to write, and I'm going use this classroom and these students as almost a kind of laboratory. I figure if I do that—they know, they can tell—it does seem to energize them. They don't feel like I'm coming in there knowing everything. We're in this together. I still have some really big questions, and that seems to encourage them to figure out what their own questions are. We use each other to try to get answers.

One of the new things I've been doing more often is that late in the process, if the student is presenting work, I'll say, "I want you to present something from your play, and I want you to think of five questions for the class about your play."

The twist is we don't actually workshop the play, we workshop the questions. I've noticed that most initial questions that we ask other people about our play are: Is it good enough? Do you like it? And they're not useful questions, really. Instead, this class session ends up getting to the heart of what you are trying to figure out in your play. Can you ask that question in a way that you can get useful feedback in the room? The truth is, if they can actually ask the question as an answerable question, I find that the students can answer it for themselves. A lot of playwriting problems—by which I mean playwriting development problems—actually come from not knowing what the question is.

This is another thing that came from the classroom into my own work as a playwright: play development becomes play development hell when—this isn't always the case—the playwright hasn't taken control of the process. The way you take control is by telling the people that you're working with—the dramaturg, the artistic director—"Here's what I'm trying to figure out with this play, and here's how you can help me." Put them to work for you. Again, this came out of being a little dissatisfied with that model where the students would bring in a couple of pages each week and then say to the room, "Do you like it? Is it good?" I just think discussions that come out of that are just opinion traffic jams. I want to empower the students.

I try to be careful about *when* I introduce structure, because I find that if you introduce it too early, students get paralyzed. But we do need to talk about it, at least in a general sense. I recently used Suzan-Lori Parks's *Father Comes Home from the Wars, Parts 1, 2, and 3* to explore structure. I taught it backwards because I wanted them to think about beginnings, middles, and endings, and to get them to think about what can you only do in a beginning? What can you only do in an ending? What can you only do in a middle? What I find fascinating about *Father Comes Home from the Wars, Parts 1, 2, and 3* is that the first play does the work of a beginning. The last play does the work of an ending. But also within the plays, you can break them down into beginnings, middles, and ends. By teaching it backwards, starting at the ending, the students become a little disoriented. Their understanding of structure is made strange again, and they become more conscious of the elements that are unique to beginning, middle, and ending.

I find myself less effective when the class is about starting from nothing. If I'm teaching a class that is about the very beginning process of making something, I'll include some sessions that are about looking at the outside world, taking something from the outside world, and internalizing it and making it your own. If they look at an outside source of inspiration and start playing with that, then they seem to be able to generate material in a way that has a sense of playfulness. My weak spot as a teacher is that I can sometimes too quickly evaporate that feeling of playfulness because I'm so analytical.

I like to have them work with some kind of source material. I do an exercise that involves reading the newspaper and finding a story that feels like it has a play in it and bringing that back, and then we work with it. Or since I've written a number plays about celebrities and historical figures, I might ask them to use a famous person as a starting place. The way that I teach that workshop involves a lot of list making. I'll have them write out things they know about this famous person—a hundred things I know about the famous person. I do have them do some work with problems and actions. I have them put a "p" by all the problems they listed, all the problems that person has, and put an "a" by all the things that person's done (accomplishments). Then I have them put a star by the problem they find most interesting, and then write about an event in their own life where they had a similar problem. I ask them to recount the memory and then write the memory as a scene. Then I have them go to a new page and write it again as a scene and just make it better. I don't say what I mean by that. It's just sort of an iterative—you did it once, just do it again. Sometimes I have people do it a third time because it often gets richer the more you just keep writing it.

So they've written a scene from their own lives, and I have them substitute in the famous person. This person takes over one of the characters. This could be you but maybe not. Then change the other person in the scene to whomever seems appropriate given who the famous person is. Then write it again, and now have it fit the famous person. It's just a merging of the personal and that which is outside you, which is the same process I have used to write a play about Isaac Newton or Walt Disney. The reason you're even thinking about that famous person, the reason you're even listing the problems you're listing has something to do with the fact that you identify with them. You find some sort of rhyme between that and your own life, so I'm just asking to merge it a bit.

I've occasionally gotten together a few of my playwright friends to have these meetings; we call them pedagogy meetings. We get together and ask, "What do we value? Can it be taught? If so, how?" It's a question of the things that we value as playwrights and determining whether they can be taught. I think building problems and actions into a play can be taught. Conflict can be taught. I find that students are really good at talking about conflict, but if you ask them to identify a moment of conflict in their play, they often can't. I think definition of conflict, to just break that down, is a character trying to do something that is difficult to do and us seeing the "trying" on stage. That is the one of the most basic definitions I can come up with.

The challenge is to show them the potential for conflict in their own work. For example, I'll take a Fornes play, remove the conflict from the scene, and then show them the scene with and without the conflict. If they can identify the difference, I take them to their own play and have them look at a moment from their own play where they're feeling it might be lacking some element of conflict or tension. Often they find that they extinguished a conflict that could have happened; in seeing a missed opportunity, they now have an idea or two or three for how expand the moment. Then they can have the experience of writing a moment of conflict, and in doing so, they really understand what conflict is, beyond merely defining it.

There is stuff that can't be taught. I always thought voice couldn't be taught, and I still kind of agree with that, but I still do that one workshop involving *Alcestis*. I don't know if that's exactly teaching voice, as much as it's actually making them sensitive to hearing the voice they have, that's useful. But I'm not doing anything that *makes* the voice. The voice is there.

In Parks's essay "Tradition and the Individual Talent" (something I often teach), she talks about her body of work and how she likes to be a little oblivious to it so as not to be a prisoner to it, but it's nonetheless there. So I like making my students a little conscious of their own body of work, if only to delight in and further indulge it or subvert it.

The other thing I think about—but this gets a little more difficult to talk about—is the drive that you need. There comes a moment in every playwriting process where the honeymoon ends. Sometimes plays run out of gas because the writers haven't done their research. I've been thinking a lot about whether research can be taught. There's a kind of notion that I think they have in mind, that everybody has in mind when they think about research. It's like … I'm writing a play about cars, so I should go research things about cars to make it more realistic.

But I think that's kind of a limited notion of research. A form of research is the work I have them do in reading other plays and breaking down how the plays work. Is there a kind of mentor play to your play that by looking at how it works, you can learn something that will unlock something in what you're writing? That will show you a pathway. If I am using a play, such as my play *The Christians*, in class, I'll spend some time showing them the point at which I realized this play is actually secretly *Antigone*, and how that helped me get to the ending, helped me toward changes I made that opened up the play. So research may be looking to another play for some kind of guidance. I always get nervous about recommending a play for them to look at, but sometimes that's my role as a teacher. I'll try to make sure that I'm not recommending just one play but I am recommending three different plays.

But then, sometimes they run out of motivation because there's something in the world of their play that remains under-explored. If there's a particular subject they're writing about, perhaps it would be useful to go out and listen to five different podcasts that will complicate their understanding of the subject. Again, the goal of the research isn't necessarily to make their rendering more "realistic," but rather to alert them to possible problems and actions related to the subject at hand that might help fuel their play and give them motivation to keep writing.

In a lot of classes, a student will be working on a play for four weeks and then say, "Can I change my play?" But oftentimes it's a bad idea for them to change it. They really have to sit with it and move through it and find that drive to fight through the relationship that's gone sour but still has potential, the fight to pass through the honeymoon phase.

My favorite solution is to ask a student to write a love letter to her play, and I'll say, "It's gotta be real—you're trying to win back your play right now—so it better be good." But still, I don't know if that drive can be taught. Perhaps that quality is what separates the students who are really going to stick with playwriting past their time of being a student and students who will let it go and do something else. You have to be obsessed.

My first obsession wasn't theater. It was theme parks. I grew up in Orlando, so I was surrounded by Disney World, which is a kind of theatrical environment, so I think in some ways that was kind of the origin. I wanted to make my own theme park. I'd even go so far as to build, for lack of a better term, theatrical installations in my bedroom, or sometimes I'd turn my room into a haunted house with hanging sheets and black lights and puppets. I think the playwriting impulse came from a kind of interest in scenic design. And in a lot of cases, that's the way that I write my plays. I start with a use of space that I find interesting, or an environment that I'd like to have built and exist in the real world.

I was dabbling in theater in high school, and I saw plays in Orlando, and then I went to college. I was going down the pre-med path, but partway through my freshman year I just found that I was writing plays in my spare time, and I moved over to the Department of Dramatic Writing at NYU. That freshman year in college I was in New York, so I was seeing Richard Foreman's work. I think that's when I first encountered Caryl Churchill's writing. Those types of things further encouraged me to explore theater.

But something in those works, especially the work of Richard Foreman, reminded me in some small way of all my childhood obsessions—obsessions with theme parks, haunted houses, magic shows. My drive to write plays is rooted in a desire to reach back to something that both frightened me and gave me a sense of wonder at a very young age. To some degree, what I'm doing now isn't that far from what I was doing in my room at age eight.

Where do you start as a playwright? You start as an audience member. I think playwrights always start as audience members. And we have, as audience members, these profound experiences in the theater; we are deeply, deeply moved, struck dumb by a play, we're amazed, and that's really, really important because it drives us to get in there and try to create for others an experience akin to the one we had. Then I think we have to also do the work of seeing past or seeing through that amazement to see how a work works.

So, first, you need to have the capacity to be amazed. And, you want to have good taste, whatever that means, and there's a wide range of what that is. Then you want to look at what you admire, and be able to see what makes it so effective ... see, with a kind of precision, what makes it worth admiring. Then you figure out where you sit with respect to those values, and you try to figure out for yourself what you uniquely value. It's that movement from another work back to your own that is crucial.

In the course of that movement, the work will change; it will mutate, it will become your own, but that's when you can step back again and say, "Does this match what I value?" Developing that skill, and really practicing it as much as you can, is vitally important.

Quiara Alegria Hudes

I don't know that writing can be taught, really, but I know bad writing habits can be taught. The most important thing is to not have a prescriptive approach to writing. There's not one way to write a play or even three ways to write a play. There are many ways to write plays, so use a diverse set of literature as your starting-off point rather than a bulleted list of what ingredients a well-made play must have.

I don't believe that there are a lot of rules. The rules were invented by people who were writing free of rules, so I don't think rules exist and are codified forever. Furthermore, it's important to consider, "How is playwriting valuable, not just to its own practice, but more broadly?"

I started playwriting as a child. It was a form of having fun, of not being bored, of enjoying the company of friends. I took a creative writing class in high school, and we submitted our ten-page plays to a contest run through Philadelphia Young Playwrights, and I won. They produced my play at Temple University. That was my first formal foray into playwriting, followed by a playwriting class at Yale when I was an undergrad. Again, this was all hobby stuff. I didn't conceive that one did such things formally. Later in my twenties, I went back to grad school to study writing, with a more serious intention. That was at Brown, with Paula Vogel. What I learned was a process of rigorous self-examination, of learning to critique one's own work lucidly, soberly, and to be competitive with oneself.

That is a hard practice. It's also rewarding, and it has a much broader application than playwriting. That practice of studying with real honesty what one has put on the page, what one feels in the heart, the challenges that remain and how to solve them, is where I try to focus my playwriting teaching. The opposite approach comes at it from an exterior point of view: "I think this scene should be that instead. I think this line should be that instead." That might yield a better second draft, but it isn't teaching the individuals the process of how to study themselves and make the work better on their own, independently.

Half of my class is a reading class. You just can't be a playwright without reading the widest breadth of playwriting, from then, from now. Playwrights need to be exposed to diverse aesthetics, in addition to the different backgrounds of the writers and characters.

My reading lists often include *Bonjour, lá, Bonjour* by Michel Tremblay and *Jerusalem* by Jez Butterworth. I do an Annie Baker. Students respond to *The Goat* by Edward Albee. *Joe Turner's Come and Gone* by August Wilson is oftentimes the most challenging one for the students, because of the baldly spiritual component of that play. (Many students seem to arrive at campus with atheist backgrounds.) I always have a Caryl Churchill. *Far Away* is a good one. I do *Glengarry Glen Ross* for talking about language plays. I try to keep them as contemporary as possible. *Buried Child* for symbolism and the gothic.

Every other week they have to read three plays. I make the three plays as different from each other as possible. I purposefully don't group them stylistically. Then we gather as a class. They come prepared, having listed the different tools that the playwright is using to dramatize his or her story. I start listing all the tools on the board. Then from the tools that they've engaged with the most, I select three tools that they have to go write a play with. Let's say, for instance, I choose direct address, no stage directions, and that the inciting incident is offstage. They have to go write a ten-page play that uses those tools. Concurrently, we look at Aristotle's six elements, especially dialogue, plot or story, and character, which are three I spend a lot of time on. I don't separate it out into distinct modules because playwriting is more fluid than that.

As students progress onto an advanced writing workshop, the reading lists become individualized, and reach further back into history. Based on what they're writing, students receive their own reading list. I take my clues from what they're writing about, what they're engaging with that they seem to also not quite have the tools for. If a student is engaging a lot with, let's say, deconstructed feminist narratives, but I can tell there's a bit of a naïve sense about it, I'll say, "Check out how these writers did that." If they're writing stoner comedy, I'll say, "Great. Check out what these authors have done. Go read some Aristophanes and see how far back the tradition goes." Oftentimes it's thematic. Oftentimes it's aesthetic. It is different from student to student.

I assign a great deal of work, and in response I have two "relief assignments" throughout the semester. One is to do a bad play festival, where I'll say, "Okay, everyone come in with five pages. The worst play you could possibly write." I've heard that Mac Wellman does this. I've heard Annie Baker and Young Jean Lee talk about "what's the play you're afraid to write?" or "what's the worst play you can possibly think of?" and it yields some wild, provocative writing. Sometimes you get great plays out of it, but mostly it's a way to remind ourselves that we can have fun. We can embarrass ourselves. It's a great group support exercise somewhere in the semester.

Conversely, in one of Sarah Ruhl's essays (from *100 Essays I Don't Have Time to Write: On Umbrellas and Sword Fights, Parades and Dogs, Fire Alarms, Children, and Theater*), she talks about how plays can be a gift. So I say, go write a play, one to ten pages, and that is a gift to these particular individuals in our workshop room. Oftentimes, these exercises come later in the semester, when we've gotten time to know each other well. The thing I like about the gift plays is that you're writing them for a specific audience and no other audience, and that yields some really beautiful, unexpected kinds of forms and types of writing.

In my first class, or in one-off teaching gigs, I dig into a three-part exercise. The first part is writing stage directions. In theatre we create illusions and tell stories. We make believe, so write a stage direction where you're not going to literally stage it, but you'll find a way to suggest it—so someone dies: a sword fight, a hurricane, that sort of thing. Then we talk about, what are plays where that happens? People bring up Shakespeare and death, and *Angels in America* and flying over the Antarctic.

The second part of the exercise asks, can you come up with a stage direction that's impossible to even represent on stage? A situation where you can't do it literally, and you can't even represent it. Then you get very philosophical responses that often have to do with the audience's experience. Recently at the Signature workshop someone said, "The audience forgets they're watching a play." That was the person's stage direction. Then we talk about it. We discuss it. How would we achieve it?

Then the third part, which to me leads to the most exciting moments of writing, is to write a stage direction where there's no artifice, zero illusion. What's happening in the story is literally what's happening on stage. Someone drinks a glass of water. Someone sweeps a floor. These sorts of literal moments ground us anew in the material world that we live in. Then make believe, the pretend, must yield to the magic of reality and of bodies on a stage. One of my favorites is: "A tailor enters, sits at a sewing machine, and begins to sew a dress." By the end of the play, the dress is complete and the lead actor puts it on. The magic of reality.

A play with no stage directions is a great language exercise, a great dialogue exercise, to really let it live. When you look at it, there are all sorts of wonderful plays without stage directions. I'm reading a Stephen Adly Guirgis play, *In Arabia We'd All Be Kings,* and there are few stage directions! There are like twelve words of stage directions the whole time. Take Caryl Churchill's *Love and Information*. She doesn't assign characters to the lines of dialogue, so there are many directions to go with no stage directions to guide. Just dialogue.

Plot is a fun one to do early on because there are many ice breaker things to do. I'll have the students choose a story we all know, like Humpty Dumpty, or the life of Jesus. Then everyone chooses one plot point, and they write a monologue during that moment in the story. Then we read those monologues chronologically. Then we'll switch up the order, follow some other plot forms. We'll read them reverse chronologically. Then we'll read them as a pattern play, so monologue one, monologue two, monologue three, monologue one, monologue four, monologue five, that sort of thing. Then we'll read them out loud as a circle play, chronologically then going back to the first one. We'll use the same writing in different ways, and it's a great, clear, fun way to talk about how structure can shed a whole different light on the same exact story, on the same exact words, and how much freedom there is in structure and how essential that is to the storytelling.

I explore character. When I was at Brown, Holly Hughes led a solo-performance workshop, and this was the first exercise: list all your identities. So what I'll do with character is have everyone write this list of identities and then read them aloud. Because I do this early in the semester, oftentimes they're very polite. They're very obvious and safe identities. If I get a group where it's "student, sophomore, soprano," I'll have them go back and write the ones that you'd rather not read out loud in this class, until we really get to a level of complexity and honesty and enigmatic nature of all the opposing identities someone can have within.

I'll scribble a few from each person on the wall. Now we've got a robust list of character traits, of identities. Then I start to talk about characters as triangles. What three things here don't go together? That would make a great character triangle. People start to call out different "character recipes." (This is a phrase that comes from Paula Vogel.) Then I have everyone decide a character triangle, on his or her own, and write a monologue from that point of view, read it out loud. Our job is to guess the character triangle from the identities listed on the board. It's Faulkner's notion that the drama is character in conflict with itself. Outside obstacles are important for characters too, but alone they do not provide sufficient depth to a play.

Dialogue can be a little bit trickier because it's hard to isolate it out of the context of a story, but I have these worksheets, and students love the worksheets because it's nostalgic from their elementary school days. I'll bring in twenty lines of very straightforward dialogue: "You're fired." "Wanna make out?" "I know you're cheating on me." Things like that. Twenty lines of that. Then they have to come up with a completely original way to say each line in a different character's voice. Then I'll go around the room, and they say their original version. We have to guess which line it was that they were saying.

The second worksheet will have a response. So, using "I know you're cheating on me," the response will be, "But I'll take you back." That sort of thing. They'll have to do responses in a different character's voice from the one they first did. This is a way to wrap our minds around the fact that sometimes the most direct way to say a line isn't necessarily the most musical or creative or fun or artistic. That provides me with a shorthand for when I am giving feedback on their plays. I say, "Remember that worksheet we did?

I think you've got something more original in you than this bit of language. Surprise me a little more here with your words." It creates a template for how to talk about language.

At least once, I have the students read their own plays aloud. It's helpful for a few reasons. One skill that's useful as a playwright is selling your own writing. Commit to the line. Say it out loud with clarity. That is actually a useful skill. Another is that when you've written a full-length play, and you have to sit there and read all those characters out loud, you can actually—now this is a muscle that one hones with practice—start to notice, "that page was really fun to read," or "that page gave me the chills," or "my mind has been wandering for the last page and a half." It's those reactions that I want the students to take note of. Most especially, when does it feel most alive? Those five pages that feel most alive? You want your whole play to feel that way. When do you check out? When do you get bored? When are you going fishing in your mind? Notice those pages. That happened for a reason too.

You'll find them noticing their own language gremlins: "Oh, I did that trick of mine eight times on that page. I can be more creative or have more variety." I see them scribbling in the margins when they don't like that line, or putting a check next to something that felt good.

I'm wary of outlining. In my screenwriting life, in my TV writing, and for musicals, I do outline, but the process of playwriting is different. I think if you know too much about your character's fate and destiny before you write it, you're not allowing yourself the freedom to learn from them. You're closing off their potential complexity. A play is much more than just plot.

Toward the end of the semester when we're rewriting, I'll have them write a self-critique, a long, engaged articulation of what they think about their play. A candid assessment. I won't give them feedback until I read their own self-critique, because I want to make sure that my criticism is steering them in a direction they're actually interested in going in. Oftentimes they'll say, "My goal is this. My goal is that. My goal is this." And I'll say, "Okay, the first two were quite evident from the writing. I had no idea about that third one, so tell me more. Go there. It's not on the page yet, so where does that live? And how can that find voice?"

One of the things Paula Vogel did was model what the life of a writer can be. I didn't have a lot of illusions graduating from Brown with my MFA, like, "Okay, now I make it as a playwright," or "Now I go pay my rent writing plays!" What she modeled for us was a little different. It was just a life of commitment, of waking up and doing it every day and of varied levels of success day-to-day, month-to-month, year-to-year. Not a job one applies for but a life one decides to live, every day. A life that includes joy and subversion. The life of a mischief maker.

Every day, while you're doing the dishes, while you're strolling to the corner store for milk, while you're falling asleep, while you're waking up, ask yourself, why does this story matter? It might be a different answer every day, but keep engaging with that. Why? Why this particular piece? Entertain yourself as much as possible during the process. Make it as complicated as possible. Be as playful as possible. Dig deep into the complication, the entertainment, the spirit of the piece. Hold oneself to the ever-deeper standard. As opposed to the high standard, I think of things getting ever deeper, always, always.

Create a very active process of self-critique, because in this world your work will be critiqued so constantly, oftentimes with vitriol, or laziness. If one has his or her own process of self-critique, it's a way to stay closer to the work, not let your ideas be blowing through the wind between all the notes and reviews you get. The self-critique can be on the line level. It can be on the scene level. It can be on the whole play level. But always be one's closest critic. That can be a loving thing. I don't think criticism is about self-loathing or being hard on oneself. It's about always examining the work, where it is now, where it can be, where you want it to be, what the questions are. Don't get comfortable. Always question, even the most basic things—*even the most basic things*—always be pushing at that boundary.

Give yourself a deadline, and have something happen at the end of that deadline. Whether it's in two weeks, "let's get together and read our new plays out loud as we eat pizza," or in two months, "oh actor friends, I'm gonna come into a rehearsal room with a play that has not yet been written as of today, and you're gonna do it." That gets the juices flowing unlike anything else.

LISA KRON

I didn't set out to be a playwright, and I didn't study play-writing—or I guess I mean to say I have no academic training in playwriting—and I don't think of myself as a particularly good teacher of playwriting, or anything else for that matter. The teachers I most admire are those with that magic (to me, anyway) ability to take their students through a progression of experiences that at some point open out into some new plane of coherence. I am not that kind of teacher. My teaching, for better and worse, reflects my scrappy and disorganized quest to understand what plays are and how they work.

How I teach and what I teach is very much a product of my own unconventional theatrical education. I often say I was trained like a vaudevillian. I was a theater major at a small Midwestern college, and right out of college I toured for a season as an actor in a national repertory company. But my true theatrical education began when I stumbled into the world of downtown theater in the East Village in the '80s and started performing nightly in the many clubs that were all over the neighborhood then.

Two things about this time really set me on my course as a playwright. One was the experience of being part of a theater collective, the WOW Café, that was a kind of bohemian community theater filled with people who were either not acquainted with or did not care about any so-called "rules" of theater. WOW was a tiny storefront theater, and there was a pay phone backstage, and it would sometimes ring during shows, and it was not unheard of for a performer to leave the stage and answer it. My college theater program had trained me in "rules" of the theater, so I knew that answering a backstage phone in the middle of a performance was not something one did in the theater—yet there was nothing I had ever seen on a stage that was as riveting.

I became fascinated with this dynamic. What did it mean to be on stage? What was the difference between actors on a stage performing for an audience and people in a room with other people? Why was it so electrifying to watch someone transition from one state to the other? This really began my obsession with parsing the dynamics of theater and ultimately influenced both my writing and my teaching.

My first solo shows were compendiums of funny, anecdotal stories, some songs—basically whatever I thought was funny. The material was all improvised in front of an audience, not written. In my first several years of performing, my quest was to figure out how to be consistently funny and how to forge an authentic and dynamic connection with an audience, which is a skill that can only be learned by actually performing in front of paying audiences. About seven years in, when I felt I had gained some mastery in those areas, I began to yearn to make work that had depth, that had an arc, a shape, work that would open out somehow into something that was more than the sum of its parts. What I was after, I know now, was dramatic action—which, I also learned, is famously difficult to achieve in a solo show.

My eureka moment came while I was working on *2.5 Minute Ride*, which was (partly) about a trip I took with my dad, a German-Jewish Holocaust refugee, to his hometown in Germany and to Auschwitz, where his parents had perished. As part of my research, I finally got around to reading T*he Diary of Anne Frank,* which is one of those books I somehow thought I knew even though I hadn't read it, which is how we are with classic books, like, you know, "I haven't read it but it's a classic, I get the gist," and then you read it and you're like, has anybody read this thing? This book is amazing!

So I read *The Diary of Anne Frank* and the thing that shocked me, the thing I didn't expect, is that she doesn't know what's going to happen. The events of the Holocaust have been described many times over, and we have this bird's-eye view. We know how things turned out, and we have a common understanding of the scope of the horror we're meant to feel. But reading Anne Frank, it dawned on me that the people living through the events we call the Holocaust of course had no bird's-eye view. These events hadn't become "events" yet. It was inchoate life, spooling forward into an unknowable future for people whose perspective is not global but emanating from their actual physical bodies. Anne Frank's fate is central to our understanding of her, but the power of her story derives from the fact that she doesn't know her fate.

For me this was a revelation: Stories and the events they describe aren't the same thing. A story is a handful of elements lifted out of that infinite swirl and presented as "what happened," but lived experience itself is not linear and has no narrative. I came to believe that this is what gives theater its particular power: it's the one narrative art form that doesn't tell "what happened" but replicates the human experience of groping our way through the ever-unfolding present toward an unknowable future. I came to believe that the trick of locating dramatic action in a solo show is that it can't be found inside the stories being recounted. Dramatically speaking, what happens in a solo show is that a person is telling a story. And if the show is to have dramatic action, the storytelling can't proceed as the storyteller intends.

Early in my teaching I had my students generate their own solo material, because that's the kind of work I'd been doing. I led them though exercises to help them break open familiar personal narratives and to locate what I called "pre-narrativized" versions of their stories—versions that moved forward in time rather than looking back. I encouraged them to develop a narrative voice that doesn't know where it's headed, that can only see as far as it can see from where it's standing at a given moment. I encouraged them to let go of omniscience, because drama is animated by the opposite of omniscience. Drama utilizes the gap between what people think is happening and what's really happening. Oedipus believes, with good reason, that he's avoided his curse. Romeo believes, with good reason, that Juliet is dead. Gripping drama is created when a play gives us the power to see what its characters cannot.

To get to this "innocent" voice, I often started with a drawing exercise from the book *The Natural Way to Draw* by Nicolaides. I asked students to choose a simple object like a coffee cup or a water bottle and draw it without looking at the paper, keeping their eyes on the object itself, moving pen on paper while feeling as if the pen was very slowly tracing the outline of the object itself. (See Nicolaides's book for a full description.)

I'd say things like: "Try to let go of the idea of what a cup is or what it looks like. Just follow the contours of this object as accurately as you can. That's your only job. The goal is not to finish, the goal is to have the experience of following the contour as searchingly as possible. Draw whatever contours you see; shadows and light are as real as anything else. Don't worry about a creating a coherent whole."

After about five or seven minutes, I would ask everyone to hold up their drawings. Sometimes it would take them a few tries to let go of drawing their idea of a cup, but when students got the hang of it, their drawings were strikingly vivid and idiosyncratic. The point of this exercise was to model the type of open-minded attention to unfolding, non-narrativized details I wanted them to find in their writing. I'm always trying to get students to work more freely and stop worrying about where they're going. I encourage them to cast around more and surprise themselves. I encourage them to try to loosen their grip on the outcome so they can look around and ask, "What is here? What's interesting about it? What can I do with what's actually here?"

I always followed that exercise with a five- or six-minute reflective writing about their experience of doing the drawing. I learned from Madeleine George that asking students to do short writings after an exercise or a discussion about what came up for them that surprised them or interested them is an extremely useful teaching tool. It gives students space and time to make their own connections between whatever they've just done and their personal writing goals.

I would often ask students to write a version of a story they'd told many times, but to use the present progressive voice—in other words, to write it moving forward in time rather than looking back. So for instance, rather than saying, "Then I went down the stairs and there was my dog, looking pleased as punch …," they'd shift to unfolding action: "I'm walking down the stairs. Oh, there's my boy, there's my Rover. Rover, no! Put down Sissy's hamster!" I encouraged them to note all of the details, whatever their attention landed on in this world they were walking through, the colors, the textures, the light, the air, the weather, the clothes, the taste in their mouth, the other people, their physical position, what they were wearing, smells, sounds.

Sometimes the details remembered were revealingly at odds with the story as they always told it: "The hamster! I'd forgotten all about the hamster! I've been so angry at Dad for driving drunk that night but I remember now, he went out to buy Sissy a new hamster."

I would ask them to notice and remove all the editorial comments, which often show up in the guise of forward movement: "My dad's breath is bad ... This will be the reason my mother will give for divorcing him ten years from now." Those sorts of comments can feel satisfying and clever, but when they're taken away, you feel the story open up into greater emotional possibility.

I had them remove conjecture and break it down into actual, granular observation. So if someone wrote, "My sister is angry," I'd say, "I don't know what that looks like. That doesn't really mean anything to me. Tell me what she's doing. What can you actually see?" This generally leads to something far more evocative, like, "Bonnie's looking out the window. Her face looks strange, empty. She's humming to herself. She's kicking the back of dad's seat. Thump, thump, thump."

I'd encourage them not to worry about contradictions, or leave things out because they don't make sense. Contradictions and mismatched details are compelling: "Ken can't drive. How is Ken driving the Impala?" It's not our job to smooth things out or make them make sense. We do ultimately want formal coherence in any work of art, but an effective form is one that gives us a means to hold and ponder the incoherence of real life.

My attention has shifted, since those early days, to another way of thinking about dramatic action. I'm now interested in thinking about transformation as the essential theatrical gesture. I haven't let go of my interest in the "innocence of the coming moment," but now I think it's the precondition for the actual event. I start this discussion in class by having my students call out examples of transformations from literature, film, or plays and making a big list on the board: Lot's wife's becomes a pillar of salt; Daryl Hannah turns from woman into mermaid back to woman in *Splash*, Midas turns all he touches to gold; Tom Hanks is suddenly a grownup in *Big*. In life we're surrounded by these instantaneous transformations, though we don't necessarily think that way: a single person is transformed into a married person; a poor person wins the lottery and becomes rich; a living person becomes dead; a childless person is suddenly a parent; a hurricane razes a town in Mississippi, etc.

What we call a dramatic event is always a transformation. Sometimes they're naturalistic, like the ones listed above, and sometimes they're fantastical: a dead person becomes a living person, or a man becomes a cockroach. Sometimes they're formal: a character who has been operating behind the fourth wall suddenly speaks to the audience. Making lists of transformations from literature helps students to trust that they don't need to fear bold, non-naturalistic choices. What could be more delightful or feel more natural than Daryl Hannah's transformations in *Splash*?

I love using a simple but powerful genre transformation exercise I got from Rob Handel. Students call out types of scenes, and someone writes them on the board: fight scene, love scene, chase scene, foreign language scene, etc. - as many kinds of scenes as they can think of. Then I have them pick a genre, doesn't matter, any genre, and begin writing a scene. Several minutes in, I tell them to switch genres. No stopping, don't overthink, just leap right into a new genre, keeping the scene rolling. Students almost always write something delightfully theatrical and alive.

When talking with students about their writing, I often ask them to tell me what transforms between the top of the play and the end. I encourage them to think of transformation as a diagnostic tool and treatment in their rewriting. 99% of inert, boring scenes are scenes devoid of transformation.

I want my students to feel unafraid to follow blind alleys, to try things, to be wrong, to experiment. Then I want them to learn to analyze the results of those experiments and craft them into a piece of theater that generates electricity between performer and audience.

I guess I'm really trying to impart two opposing ideas. One is that they need to let go of their logical mind, to hurl themselves with abandon into feeding their own aesthetic curiosity, to become attuned to the strangeness of their own minds and to learn the delight of following the scent of some compelling image or juxtaposition that is calling to them from just outside the borderline of their comprehension. And then I want them to master the craft of taking all of that pulsing, living strangeness and shaping it into coherence—not logic, not resolution, but coherence on its own terms.

When I was in my twenties, many people I knew were skeptical of craft, believing it led to formulaic work and canned narratives. They felt its purpose was to stifle wildness, contradiction, and unpredictability. But the old saw is right: real craft is freedom. It's not a map. It's still an intuitive process. There's no destination that anyone else can point you toward. But to know theatrical craft is to have the ability to employ our art form's particular mechanisms of dynamic engagement with an audience. If you learn the dynamic principles of dramatic action, and you learn to recognize and manipulate various forms and tropes, you can make something that feels very alive. You can put anything you want inside those mechanisms—anything you wonder about and feel a need to wrestle with.

For me, the process of finding the form or shape of a play is an almost visceral experience. I have an actual physical sensation of projecting myself through space, peering down halls, and looking around the corners of the play, listening for something alive, something stirring, something outside me, crazier than me, more complicated than me, something that's in a state of tension, change, or flux, and then building a shape for the play that will let that flux play itself out in the most complete way possible. This is not easy to teach, but I try to guide my students toward an aggressively curious pursuit of their own work and to have them take on the challenge of bravely allowing each play to become what it needs to be instead of what the writer (or director, dramaturg, or producer!) would prefer it to be.

I spend a lot of time with my students talking about plays they've seen or read. I really encourage them to respond with what I think is called in literature a "believing reading," meaning you respond to a piece with the assumption it's a coherent piece of work and your job is to respond on its own terms rather than what we all usually do which is to project our own playwriting impulses onto someone else's work. I want my students to develop a sophisticated understanding of formal difference in plays. This work of looking for a core of intention in the work of others is key, I think, in helping them locate the core of intention in their own work, to learn to defend it from the misguided dramaturgy they no doubt have already encountered and will continue to encounter throughout their careers.

I always want my students to locate their passion as writers. Part of every class is spent having them do free-writings on prompts to that end. For instance, in an exercise inspired by Ken Prestininzi, I'll have them write about the plays they love the most and why they love them and the plays they hate the most and why they hate them and then to think about what that tells them about what kind of plays they want to write. I'll ask them to write about things they've seen on stage that raised the bar for them in terms of what they want to make in their own work, things that made them yearn to do better. I offer examples from my own life and work, for instance:

- Watching Deb Margolin on stage at the Wawa Hut in the 1980s. Noticing her ability to be very funny and then suddenly opening into a kind of fathomless depth of feeling, and realizing I had no idea how to do that but I wanted to.
- Noticing Brecht's lack of agenda in *Good Person of Szechwan* and his willingness to show his characters in all their complexity and ugliness, to not protect them from the audience's judgment. Yearning to be able to write characters that fearlessly, with that level of honesty and human complexity.
- Marveling at the fantastical, non-linear leaps Ethan Lipton makes in the lyrics to his song "Greg Aguilera." Wondering how he does it. Wondering where that kind of fantastical imagery comes from.

I now start every class I teach by reading and discussing Thornton Wilder's essay "Some Notes on Playwriting" from his book *American Characteristics*. I'm only being slightly hyperbolic when I say that there's nothing a playwright needs to know about plays that's not contained in that essay.

I've recently started having students read the first ten pages or so of *Our Town* aloud in class, and then I ask them to identify every theatrical move they can find. Wilder sucks us in so quickly it can be hard to notice how many ways he transforms the relationship of that speaker to the audience, or how effortlessly he draws us into Grovers Corners, then slips back out to show us it's all artifice, and then slips us right back inside again. It's so deft we don't even feel ourselves crossing back and forth from one state to another, but it's those rapid-fire theatrical transformations that make the play one of the most compelling ever put on a stage. The opening monologue is basically a lesson in theatrical engagement.

I want my students to trust their own imaginations, their own impulses, and their own voices. I want them to understand there's no right way to write a play. There's not even a better way to write a play. If they have an idea or a vision, they should go for it. "That will never work" is nonsense. An initial idea is nothing really, it's all about where the writer takes that idea. I want my students to take charge of that process. But I come across too many students trying to figure out how to write a play that will be acceptable, looking for permission and approval. I try to break them of that habit. Some are wrestling with absurd "rules" for playwriting they've picked up along the way, and every playwright has received terrible dramaturgy. Good dramaturgy is invaluable but one of the rarest things on earth, I'm afraid. I want my students to learn to nod and smile when they receive bad dramaturgy, and then kick it to the curb.

I feel sometimes that students now are almost too deferential to craft—or rather to an idea of craft that is something outside them that can be told to them by someone else. I want my students to be fierce. I want them to know what their own aesthetic and thematic preoccupations are so they can fight for them. I want them to tell anyone who gives them shitty notes about their plays to fuck off. I want them to want to write better and different from anyone else. I want them to want to "reinvent" theater so I can feel irritated at them for being so naïve. I want them to understand that the primary relationship of any playwright is not with an artistic director, it's with the audience.

This leads to the thing I'm currently most interested in conveying to my students: a sense of ownership of their own process. Recent free-writing topics have been along the lines of:

- What's the ideal theater where your thesis play will be done?
- What is the physical layout of the building? The configuration of the theater, the lobby, the backstage, the outside of the building?
- What kind of an environment? Where, geographically? (e. g., strip mall? Forest?)
- What's your ideal of what your writing life will be—not what you think is possible, not what you might cobble together, but your ideal?

I have them identify all the theaters across the country producing new plays. I have them research what kinds of plays each of those theaters is producing and then decide which theaters are producing work that is in conversation with their own writing. And then we brainstorm ways they might build a relationship with that theater.

There are definitely aspects of playwriting that can be taught. Can anybody write a play? Probably not. You have to be observant and have a point of view. You need, definitely need, curiosity. It helps to have a sense of humor. Mostly you have to be interested in flux more than you are interested in stasis. You have to be drawn to places where things are unsettled.

CARLOS MURILLO

What I enjoy most about teaching playwriting is witnessing the transformative power the work has on my students. As undergraduates in a theater conservatory, they're an idiosyncratic group of young people who around age seventeen, self-selected to become playwrights. In a world where there are countless (and far more lucrative) delivery systems for telling stories, I'm moved by these young people who believe in the power of theatrical storytelling and are committed enough to pursue it as a vocation. I'm catching them in a key period of time when they are in the throes of forging their identities as young artists and young adults awakening to the power of their own agency in the world, so it's thrilling to guide them over four years as they grapple with process, moving from early tentativeness and uncertainty to a place where they develop confidence and a degree of mastery over their voices and visions.

When they graduate, they go on to follow a broad range of pursuits—of course many continue their pursuit of playwriting, but others take paths that lead elsewhere (usually to interesting places). Either way, their experience learning the 3D chess-like process of writing plays serves them well—they leave The Theatre School with high-level problem-solving skills, a deep understanding and appreciation of process, the ability to follow through on projects from concept to rollout, and most importantly, a heightened sense of empathy and humanity that comes with rendering on stage what it means to be alive on earth.

I pursued an unusual path on my journey to becoming a playwright and teacher. I don't have an MFA—in fact, my traditional educational path came to an end in the late '80s when I left Syracuse University after my first year in the BFA acting program. I remember a particular acting teacher of mine offering feedback on a scene performed by one of my peers. He talked about how the work was devoid of risk—and that risk was key to making good art. I sensed a dissonance between his words and the picture I was seeing—him sitting in his chair, a bit self-satisfied, taking pleasure in an easy takedown of a young, vulnerable student. On my way home, I kept thinking, *What is the riskiest thing I can do right now in my life?*

The next day I went to the College of Arts and Sciences and filled out my withdrawal papers, much to the chagrin of my immigrant parents, who themselves lacked degrees and prided themselves on raising four children who were first-generation college graduates.

After leaving Syracuse, I traveled for a while, spent a semester at the National Theatre Institute of the O'Neill Center, where I first really caught the playwriting bug, and moved to New York. The subsequent years I describe as my "medieval apprenticeship" years—or my matriculation in the College of Hard Knocks. I spent a year at Circle Rep doing an internship in stage management, followed by a season interning with the artistic staff at New York Theatre Workshop. I had the privilege of witnessing Anne Bogart and Paula Vogel collaborate on *The Baltimore Walt,* Caryl Churchill, Mark Wing-Davey, and Lisa Peterson remount *Owners* and *Traps* in rep. I studied with Maria Irene Fornes, Jean Claude van Itallie, and Anne Bogart. I was hired by Morgan Jenness to work in the literary office at the Public Theatre during the first two seasons of George C. Wolfe's tenure there. I assisted Robert Woodruff and studied with Eduardo Machado under the auspices of the Public's Emerging Playwrights Unit. All the while I was staging small productions of my own plays in small downtown spaces in the Lower East Side. In 1995, I started to get recognition for my own writing through South Coast Rep's Hispanic Playwrights Project and when I received a Jerome Fellowship at the Playwrights' Center in Minneapolis. Then life happened.

When I first started teaching, I wasn't convinced that the art and craft of playwriting was teachable. Early on I felt very dubious about my own abilities, that I was cheating my students because every time I sat down to write a play—even after having written many of them—I felt as lost, confused, and ill-equipped to accomplish the task as they likely felt. A couple of years in I started to ask myself: When you are writing well, what is actually happening to you? I asked this of my students—their answers echoed my own: they felt like they were inside of the world they were writing; they felt like they were "channeling" something; they heard voices and saw images unfold faster than they could type; they felt like moving around; time disappeared; they experience "flow"; they breathed like their characters; they felt like some powerful force beyond them was in control. I was struck by the mystical quality of the language they used—and by extension, how near impossible it is to conjure mystical experiences at will. Which led to a question that has shaped my work as a teacher since: How do I create for my students a space in which replicating these experiences is possible and repeatable?

I imagine each student playwright as a unique organism in possession of his or her own distinct, singular voice, sensibility. and way of seeing, waiting to be coaxed out. Perceiving them that way helps me define my job, which is to guide them to write the plays that only they can write. I am very much against the idea of putting an aesthetic stamp on my writers or trying to constrain them with received notions about form and content. Our success as a program is best reflected in the wide stylistic bandwidth of work that's come out of it over the years—from experimental plays to psychologically driven kitchen sink dramas, from poetic language-driven works to socially and politically engaged calls to action, and everything in between. This variety arises from an organic approach to teaching the craft of playwriting—which entails listening to the student, individually tailoring pedagogy to meet the needs of each student's particular trajectory, designing workshops to address the specific worlds of each play, and providing each student with relevant existing models from the worlds of dramatic literature, cinema, music, the plastic arts, and other literary and performance genres.

Playwriting students at The Theatre School begin the trajectory of their majors in their second year, after a freshman foundational year in which they study theater history, criticism, and performance. In their second year, playwrights first study with my colleague Dean Corrin, who founded the program in the '90s and was a long-time ensemble playwright at Victory Gardens Theater. Through a series of well-crafted exercises, he teaches fundamentals—conflict, subtext, dramatic action, etc., which culminate in a sequence of short scenes and ten-minute plays.

In winter quarter they take my class. We focus primarily on character and world development through a sequence of exercises I've evolved over the years that have their ancestral roots in the teaching of Maria Irene Fornes, who I studied with in my own formative years as a playwright. My students often hear from me the constant refrain "characters have bodies." While a self-evident concept, I find that it challenges students in profound ways, as it forces them to stretch their imaginations beyond their own physical boundaries and sense of self into the physical experiences of other bodies and the language and worldviews that stem from them. I believe in the symbiotic relationship between the body and the voice, which of course is the foundation of most voice and speech training for actors. Language is rooted in physical impulses and needs, so it behooves us as writers in a form that uses spoken language as the primary tool to vividly imagine the bodily experience of the characters who speak those words.

An example that I use that helps students grasp this concept is describing my experience witnessing the process of language development with my own children. As infants, expression is limited to sounds of pleasure and sounds of distress—the latter usually related to sleepiness, hunger, or other discomforts. As the infant develops and gains mastery over his or her body, this is accompanied by increasing sophistication in the sounds the child makes until amorphous sounds coalesce into words. Extending that idea further, I play a thought experiment with the students: How might a child's language development be impacted by differing circumstances in how he or she was reared? Would a child who is neglected, shut down by a caregiver, develop language differently than, say, a child who is overprotected and coddled? Implicit in this thought experiment is one of the key tools for a playwright: having the capacity to imagine oneself in the body of another and discovering the language that comes from it.

The first exercise: I ask students to come up with a list of ten to fifteen alternative names for themselves. The guiding principle for choosing the names is the following: imagine the different personas you inhabit in different circumstances and moments in your life—for example, who is the you on a first date? Who is the you when you are on a vacation with your family? Who is the you when you are jealous or angry or in love? Is there an aspect of your personality that is still an adolescent? Is there a crotchety eighty-five-year-old curmudgeon lurking inside you? Is there more than one gender, sexual orientation, or ethnicity cohabiting within the multiple personas that comprise your character? Do magical beings or superheroes or supernatural or superstar figures coexist with the ordinary and mundane? I encourage my students to think beyond the pedestrian and expand their imaginative limits when conceiving these alternate names.

The second step of the exercise: find visual images corresponding to each persona. If each of these people existed in the world as autonomous beings, what would they look like? What sort of clothes do they wear, how do their bodies inhabit space? This dossier of images forms the basis of a sequence of writing exercises aimed at generating characters, worlds, and the seeds of a play.

As an example, I'll outline a common first exercise. At the top of class, I invite the students to create their own private writing spaces (we're blessed to work in large acting studios, so we are not limited by desks). Once in place, I ask the students to choose a name/image from their dossier—preferably a persona that feels very distant from them that day. I have them spend time studying the image closely, making note of every apparent and implied detail they can extract from it. I then talk the students through a sensory exploration in which they imagine what transformations their own bodies would have to undergo in order to inhabit the body of their persona/image. From there they explore physicality and movement: How does this person move through space? What do their legs, arms, spines, feet, faces feel like? Taken together, how do these physical sensations shape the sounds made by the voice? After ten to fifteen minutes of this, we begin to write.

The first prompt I throw their way, I ask them to fully imagine the character's experience of the first time they thought they were in love. This prompt is followed by sensory prompts—what were the air and the light like, where are you, what colors do you see, smells you smell, etc.? From there they begin to write, followed by more prompts and explorations of strong sensory/emotional experiences aimed to developing a sense of the character as a *person* autonomous from themselves. From these classroom exercises the students then go off and build scenes from the material they generated. For a few weeks we continue these types of exercises, after which the students choose the material that most interests them (more often than not they draw on and synthesize material from several exercises) that they will pursue for the remainder of the quarter toward writing a long one-act, first act of a longer play, or if they are super ambitious, a full-length work.

In Michelle Memran's documentary film about Maria Irene Fornes, *The Rest I Make Up*, Edward Albee talks about Irene's writing process, saying that she "figured out the play she wanted to write by writing it." I believe this is a really useful way of thinking about playwriting—not only as a professional in the field, but for a student learning the craft in the classroom, as it lends itself to an organic process, steers the writer away from clichés and contrivance. In my early days as a teacher a decade and a half ago, I often encountered students who would describe at length their ideas for plays they wanted to write. They were often highly detailed, contained wild dramatic turns, and were packed with all sorts of complicated ideas and twists.

I'd say, "Great, go and write that." Almost to a playwright, they would run out of steam within a couple of weeks and ultimately stop working on the play and switch over to a new idea. I wondered why this would happen so often—and from diagnosing the problem with students, it became clear that whatever they ended up putting on paper never lived up to the imaginary play that existed in their heads. I found that when I switched to a more organic approach, where we set aside preplanning and predetermination, students became much more engaged, surprised by what they were writing, and more fully motivated to engage in the long and challenging process toward completing a play.

This organic approach to teaching how to write a play mirrors what filmmaker David Lynch described what creativity is in an interview with Paul Holdengräber for *Live from the NYPL*: Ideas "are beautiful gifts. And I always say, you desiring an idea is like a bait on a hook—you can pull them in. And if you catch an idea that you love, that's a beautiful, beautiful day. And you write that idea down so you won't forget it. And that idea that you caught might just be a fragment of the whole—whatever it is you're working on—but now you have even more bait. Thinking about that small fragment—that little fish—will bring in more, and they'll come in and they'll hook on. And more and more come in, and pretty soon you might have a script—or a chair, or a painting, or an idea for a painting."

Theatre School playwrights spend the entirety of their third year writing a full-length play—a process that requires a different mind-set and level of commitment than the shorter works they write in the second year. I divide the year into three distinct phases that correspond to our three-quarter academic year. I am able to put a name to these phases thanks to an attorney-playwright I met in Florida about a decade ago who was enrolled in a master class I was teaching. At the conclusion of the workshop, which met three weekends over a calendar year, he said my approach reminded him of an essay he'd read by Betty Sue Flowers—a former professor of English at UT Austin and former director of the LBJ Library and Museum—titled "Madman, Architect, Carpenter, and Judge: Roles and the Writing Process." The essay, intended for students of expository writing, breaks down the writing process into the four distinct phases from the title, arguing that writers experience blocks when "competing energies lock horn to horn." As an example in her essay, she talks about the madman's conflicts with the judge—madman is chock "full of ideas, writes crazily and perhaps rather sloppily, gets carried away by enthusiasm or anger, and if really let loose, could turn out ten pages an hour," whereas the judge will hold such impulses in check, being "educated and knows a sentence fragment when he sees one. He peers over your shoulder and says, 'That's trash!' with such authority that the madman loses his crazy confidence and shrivels up." In my design of the course, I separate the competing impulses of madman (the unfiltered generator of chaos), architect (the organizer and maker of blueprints from chaos), carpenter (the detail oriented executor of the architect's plans), and judge (the perfectionist) in order to keep students on task and not fall victim to writing paralysis when those competing impulses collide against each other.

The first seven weeks of autumn quarter focuses on the madman phase—I encourage students to make a huge mess, follow every writing impulse, image, idea that comes to them. I give them permission to write unfiltered and to silence any inner critical judgment of what they write. At week three, patterns naturally begin to arise from the chaos—characters, worlds, language patterns, themes emerge, even if they are not conscious of it.

The madman phase is driven by a repertoire of exercises I've developed over the years and continue to evolve. In the last three years or so I've kicked off the class by sharing an amazing BBC audio piece by writer and poet Deborah Lavey called *The Glass Piano*, which tells the fascinating true story of nineteenth-century Princess Alexandra Amelie of Bavaria. The princess lived her life believing she had swallowed a glass piano. The story is useful in class for two reasons: one, it is brilliantly told, employing multiple storytelling modes: documentary, first-person narrative, dramatic reenactments, and a gorgeous soundscape and score. It achieves a striking balance between classical and experimental forms. Second, the story emphasizes the experience of the body. The body is key to the story—here we have a character who believes she has swallowed a glass piano and is thus forced into navigating the world with this curious physical obstacle. This condition impacts everything in her life—how she moves, how she relates to her physical environment and other human beings, and how she perceives herself. Furthermore, it illustrates the symbiotic relationship between a person's psyche, how the person experiences his or her body, and how this shapes the person's language.

After listening to the story we write, I ask the students to write up a list of possible non-normative bodily experiences. These can range from real-world examples, such as, say, a soldier missing a limb or someone suffering a debilitating malady, to more fantastical examples—what if you imagined a person with spider legs for fingers, or someone whose skin is made from plastic?

After generating a long list, I then ask the students to write a corresponding list describing the opposite experience. For example, the opposite of spider-finger man might be the satin-gloved debutante. For the next hour or so, students write speculative plays inspired by the lists. As their weekend assignment, students generate fifteen to twenty pages of new material borne out of the exercises that we read and discuss in class. In those early discussions, I avoid traditional dramaturgical language in the sense that we don't talk about what "works"—the conversations are more focused on images and moments that have resonance that might be seeds for bigger ideas.

This year I introduced the students to Italo Calvino's collection *Italian Folktales* to illustrate that logic in storytelling need not be confined to psychological consistency or rational a+b=c cause and effect. One story we read tells the story of a king's daughter who goes missing. A sea captain volunteers to find her but can't recruit any seamen to join him, until the town drunk arrives and joins up. At sea, the drunk misbehaves so much that the captain dumps him overboard. The drunk ends up on the island and rescues the princess after defeating a magic octopus. Princess and drunk are rescued by the captain that left them for dead. As they head back to port, the captain plies the drunk with liquor and tosses him overboard again so he can claim the rescue and win the princess as his bride. Returning home, the sea captain is about to marry the princess when the drunk, now a seaweed-clad monster, appears at the wedding to make his rightful claim on the princess's hand. The story eschews psychology and rationality and seems constructed as a sequence of random events. But another kind of logic—perhaps the logic of magic and dreams—gives it a coherence and power that staggers the reader.

Fear and anxiety exist at the core of the story—the inciting incident is a father terrified by the loss of his daughter. All the wild, improbable twists and turns stem from that fear and anxiety all the way through the story's resolution—a strange wedding. It's a journey from fear to the conquering of the fear. Objects play a significant role in the story—for example, there's a ring that is exchanged between the king's daughter and the drunk when they first meet, which later reappears in the climax, precipitating the story's final, decisive twist. Translated to an exercise: make a catalogue of possible fears—from the rational (the outcome of the 2016 election) to the irrational (I will wake up one morning and realize I turned into a cockroach overnight). Make a corresponding catalogue of what would eradicate those fears. Imagine a sequence of objects that might be key in a journey from fear to the absence of that fear. Avoid the logic of psychology or cause and effect. Write twenty pages.

As we get further in the quarter, the exercises shift from the purely generative to ones that nudge students to start thinking about longer sequences of action and possible forms for their plays. One exercise I like to do is to bring in the opening scenes of about a dozen plays across a wide spectrum of styles and eras—everything from ancient Greek drama to experimental stuff to kitchen sink realism and everything in between. From closely analyzing these scenes, what expectations do they set up in terms of action, character, world creation, etc.? What implications are built into those scenes that suggest sequences of action that might follow? What rules and questions are embedded in each scene's construction? Turning this analysis back to the students' work, I challenge them with an assignment: based on the material you've written thus far, and knowing what you know about the worlds you are writing about, write five possible first scenes for your play.

Taking it further, I borrow a page from Elinor Fuchs's essay on reading plays, "Visit to a Small Planet." I'll assign a play—this year I chose Caryl Churchill's *Mad Forest*—and have the students create a storyboard of sorts, starting with the first image of the play and the final image of the play. They then select a sequence of key images from the play that are gateways from that first moment to the final moment. Again, turning back to their own work, I ask them to view the material they've written to that point through the same lens. What is the first image? What might be a possible last image implied by that first one? Can you imagine a sequence of key images that will take us from beginning to end?

The shift from unfiltered material generated in the madman phase thus organically shifts—the students begin to think architecturally about their work. This usually happens around week seven. Students begin to look at the irrational mass of material written over the previous weeks through the rational eyes of the architect. The architect searches for patterns in the raw material, elements that suggest story, and sequences of action and thematic commonalities, and from those selects material to shape into an early blueprint of what will eventually become a play. At the end of the quarter, students are expected to turn in a ninety-three-page (the number is totally arbitrary) prototype of a possible first draft.

In winter we continue as architects and transition to carpentry. Winter quarter is the most challenging period of the sequence as the writers grapple with transforming the material from fall into something that resembles a first draft of the play—or what I call draft .7. It's especially challenging because the novelty of the madman quarter has worn off, leaving them vulnerable to self-doubt and second guessing. Many of the students will have the impulse to jump ship and start on something new. I have a hard and fast rule that they must follow through with what they started, and learn to love the difficult process of shaping their play from these raw materials. They're faced with making big decisions about their plays, and the process becomes less about writing toward the assignments I give them and more about making writing and rewriting part of their daily practice. Each student has multiple class sessions devoted solely to their plays over winter quarter, and I try my best to tailor those sessions to address the needs of each individual writer and play. I encourage the students to have agency in their process—what do they need from the sessions that will help their projects move forward? Sometimes that will entail table work sessions, other times we'll invite actors into the room to play with scenes on their feet. Other times the playwrights will bring in research materials for discussion or bring in improvisation scenarios to explore ideas they haven't put to paper yet. Improvisation can be a useful tool as I find it common that students will write a scene where not much is happening, but as they get further along, they'll come to a moment of real drama, only to stop before it plays out. "Let's imagine that last moment as the beginning of the scene," I'll suggest as a frame for an improvisational exploration. Building improvs from these "stem cell moments of drama," as I call them, can open up possibilities that they could not access when sitting home alone writing on their laptops.

Winter quarter I will also assign readings specifically tailored to each writer. These aren't necessarily plays—I might point them to novels, music, visual art, or films that might be relevant to what they are grappling with vis-à-vis their plays. These reading assignments tend to be fairly spontaneous. A writer might be struggling with a formalistic question that will remind me of a particular song or work of art that might help guide them to a solution. Other times it's related to a playwrights' sensibility—knowing there are other works and artists out there who are simpatico with their own work can be really helpful, even if it is just a reminder that they are not alone in their aesthetic preoccupations or in tackling difficult subject matter. One student a few years ago was working on a play about an aging female hoarder—I recommended he watch the Maysles brothers' film *Grey Gardens*. A female student working on a coming-of-age play about a female poet watched, on my suggestion, Kenneth Lonergan's film *Margaret*, which helped her reframe her thinking about some of the dynamics in her play. These suggestions are not meant to encourage mimicry—rather, they provide students with models to juxtapose their work to develop more refined and specific thinking about it.

At the end of winter quarter, we do "Day of Plays" a marathon day of unrehearsed readings of the plays in whatever shape they are in at that point. Students are required to cast the parts on their own, drawing from The Theatre School acting company. We get together at eight in the morning and read all day, eat lots of snacks, until we're done, sometimes twelve hours later. It's as much a community building event for the writers as it is a milestone along what has to this point been an intense twenty weeks. It also sets us up for spring quarter, where we'll engage in further carpentry and transition to the judge phase.

Spring quarter is dominated by visual mapping, a technique I first became familiar with thanks to the director Lisa Peterson, who I first got to work with in 1996 at the Sundance Theatre Lab on an early play of mine called *Schadenfreude*. During the workshop I hit a stumbling block in the second act—I couldn't identify what wasn't working, so Lisa pulled out a stack of index cards and wrote the main actions of each scene on individual cards and posted them up on a wall. Things ran very smoothly—each scene had a clear line of action, and each one seemed to dovetail nicely into the next … that is until we reached the problem point. Suddenly, instead of having one card to represent the action of the problem scene, there were about five or six—all posted on top of each other. It was as if the play was rolling smoothly down the highway only to suddenly find itself in the thick of a twenty-car pileup. You could *see* it on the wall—there was visual proof right there of what was making the play go off the rails. It revealed to me not only the problem but what needed to happen to correct it.

Building on this foundation, I teach my students an expanded version of mapping, where we create thick, layer cake-like maps of their plays that track every character, how space evolves over time, the trajectory of objects, thematic development, and the movement of time itself. Each student is assigned a track—students assigned to follow individual characters are tasked with identifying where they are at the beginning of each scene and how they change by the end, using active language. At first they struggle a bit finding good verbs to describe the actions in the scenes—but by the end of the quarter, they're conjuring up great and super vivid verbs. We take a lot of time—sometimes two or three class sessions (nine hours) to cover one play thoroughly. The map ends up containing a ton of information—the playwrights can see problem areas: Why does the protagonist disappear for this whole section? Is this particular sequence of events in the right place? Why does this scene devoid of action need to be in the play? You introduce this key object here; why does it never return? Armed with this wealth of information, the playwrights dive into rewrites in preparation our annual new plays festival Wrights of Spring. From the pool of plays presented in the festival we select the ones that will go on to full production in the playwrights' fourth year.

This model has been very successful over the years. Many excellent plays have arisen from this process, and the students leave third year with a deeper understanding of process. Perhaps most important, over the year we forge a community of writers who become as invested in the growth and success of their peers as they are in the development of their own work. They build relationships that sustain them through the isolating process of writing and will often transcend their time at The Theatre School.

I also teach Playwrights' Seminar, a class about form for second- and third-year playwrights. They take it twice, so I change it up from year to year. Unlike the impulse-driven, free-associative work of the third year, this course focuses on formal constraints as a way into writing plays. The most recent iteration of the class centered on the problem of writing historical lives for the stage. I've written numerous plays that deal with historical figures. In doing so I vigorously avoid the clichéd Hollywood biopic model, believing that the form of a theatrical treatment of biographical/historical matter should reflect its subject—in the way that Frank Lloyd Wright believed that a building should be an organic outgrowth and reflection of the environment and site on which it is built. Put another way, every historical life has unique contours, so the shape of a play about it should be unique to its subject. I build the course around a body of work by artists in all disciplines who have grappled with biographical/historical subject matter in unique and often boundary pushing ways.

At the beginning of the course, students select a historical figure they will spend the quarter working on. Each week I share with the students a different work that has a unique angle in handling its subject. Some examples: Robert Wilson's and Philip Glass's treatment of Einstein in their groundbreaking opera *Einstein on the Beach*; Roger Guenveur Smith's jazz-influenced solo performance, *A Huey P. Newton Story*; Bob Dylan's early '60s topical songs and their folk antecedents; *Power Goes*, The Seldoms' dance-theater piece that uses LBJ and Obama as springboards for a meditation on the nature of power; Adrienne Kennedy's collision of autobiography and Hollywood icons in her play *A Movie Star Has to Star in Black and White*; Todd Haynes's *Superstar*, a pseudo-documentary/movie-of-the-week-with-Barbie-doll depiction of Karen Carpenter. After encountering these works, students reverse-engineer them, extracting formal vocabularies and storytelling strategies employed by the artists. Using these vocabularies and strategies as the basis for their own writing experiments, each week they write ten-page, form-driven "prototype" bio-plays on their subjects. By the end of the quarter they complete ten of these prototype plays.

In alternate years I teach another version of the class that uses architectural theory as the starting point for studying and understanding form. We read Le Corbusier, Louis Sullivan, Mies van der Rohe, Rem Koolhaas, and others. Collectively, their writings grapple with the problem of creating unified and innovative works from the multiple and often competing interests and needs that drive any design process. For example, we study Dutch architect Rem Koolhaas's extraordinary CCTV Tower in Beijing. Koolhaas faced the daunting task of coming up with a design that could a) synthesize under one roof the entire massive operation of China's largest media company (once housed across numerous buildings); b) organize a program where the multiple parts of the operation exist in relationship to each other that would maximize efficiency while anticipating exponential growth; and c) serve as an international icon for a new, globally oriented Chinese state. Koolhaas came up with a radical design—instead of building a vertical structure (which would have been taller than the Freedom Tower), he reinvented the skyscraper by folding the structure in on itself into the shape of a circular box. The building's radical and singular shape is not merely the product of a starchitects' "look at me" gesture, – it is the outcome of deep thinking about the building's purpose, program, and meaning to the society that built it. The building is a staggering work that redefines what an office building can be, but in a completely rational, well-thought-out way driven by carefully articulated questions and solutions.

To me, this is directly applicable to play construction: When you are organizing your play, what questions are you asking of your materials? Why are you putting it together the way you are putting it together? How does the play's purpose (or multiple purposes) drive your decisions when it comes to form?

When the students enter their fourth year, I am very hands off. By the time they've reached their fourth year, they have undergone a cognitive shift about what it means to be a playwright. Until their third year, students tend to write toward assignment—to fulfill the course requirements, to please the professor, etc. At some point this shifts: writing becomes part of their daily practice, and their will to write is less about external validation and more about an inner drive to solve the mystery of their play. Having developed an independent artistry, I become, happily, somewhat redundant to my students and am able to create a space for them where they are exposed to a wide variety of voices and approaches. One of the great things about being in Chicago is that I'm able to capitalize on the depth of our theater community and hire really wonderful artists to work with my playwriting students.

I started teaching as the practical life thing of trying to earn a living. I not only fell in love with the process, I see it as vital to my own practice as a playwright. The day-to-day engagement with my students grappling through a writing process feeds me and teaches me as I grapple with my own. The last couple of full-lengths I've written happened to coincide with the time frame my students were working on their own. This timing has been fortuitous for me and my students—for me, I am reminded of each discreet phase of the process, and the students, I believe, take comfort in the fact that their professor is dealing with many of the same questions they are.

I try to create a space that encourages students to maximize their creative potential and challenges them to be rigorous, passionate, and steadfast in their work while also aiming to build a strong community of writers who are invested in each other's success. It's a vital, lively room to be in day after day. Over the years, the work of my students has gotten stronger and stronger because of improvements I make to the curriculum based on these values. My students, when they graduate, follow really interesting paths. I'm equally proud of my writers who go on to make a mark in the theater as I am of others who end up in a different field but use the process-oriented skills they learned while crafting play worlds of their own. In the end, that is what I teach—process and loving all the effort, trial, error, discovery, and euphoria that comes when you start with nothing, a blank page, maybe some ideas in your head and journey toward complete thing. I believe that is a hugely valuable life lesson.

SUZAN-LORI PARKS

Some Notes on Teaching Writing

DISCLAIMER

I start my writing classes by informing my students that I don't have a degree in writing; I didn't go to a writing school. I did go to college (Mount Holyoke, where I studied English and German literature). Along the way I've have had great teachers and mentors, including James Baldwin. But I haven't attended a creative writing program.

Most everything I've learned about writing I've learned by doing, by living the artist's life, by "hanging out on the street corner," as we say. I feel that while an academic degree in writing may be helpful, the real learning of writing comes from a rigorous, steadfast, and modest dedication to the doing of it and by exposing yourself to the arts, reading widely, seeing shows, etc. And to nest a disclaimer within this disclaimer, I have, since becoming a recognized professional in the field, taught at many colleges and universities. So, yeah, go figure. Can writing be taught? Maybe. Can writing be learned? You betcha. I have a yoga practice, and we say, "the practice is the teacher." Same with writing. Perhaps the blank page has taught me almost everything.

*

QUESTIONS AND CHALLENGES

How do we keep writing when we have a day job? How do we take notes from lovely and intelligent people who don't seem to get our work at all? How do we deal with good reviews? Bad reviews? No reviews? How do we deal with an artistic institution or publisher or producer who we feel wants us to be a token? What do we do when we're excluded? How do we deal with our anger? Pride? Ego? Envy? Sloth? Desire? How do we find our voice? How do we deal with a voice that changes? How do we deal with our own success? How do we continue without tripping on ourselves? How to we deal with the success of others when our own work seems to be "going nowhere"? How do we continue in the face of despair? It's important to ask the questions. It's important to bear witness to the challenges.

Sᴜꜱᴛᴀɪɴᴀʙʟᴇ Pʀᴀᴄᴛɪᴄᴇ

While I'm interested in helping my students improve their writing, I am more interested in helping them create a sustainable artistic practice. Writing something is a one-time thing, but a writing practice is a lifelong thing. Here are some ways to create sustainability:

1. Meditation Practice: If you don't already have one, begin one today. There are lots of great meditation teachers and programs and books out there. Begin (or re-begin) today.

2. Embrace a Physical Practice: Being an artist is a full-body thing. Yoga, running, swimming, surfing, walking, dancing, martial arts, cycling—whatever, that is physical and regular.

3. Mental Chatter: Become aware of yours. Get a handle on your self-talk. If your self-talk is predominately negative, then please wake up to that. If your self-talk is only positive and doubts that you or your work are candidates for improvement or expansion, then wake up to that. In Sanskrit it's called Svadhyaya: "reading yourself" or "self-study."

4. Your News Feed: Monitor this. No need to constantly be checking your social media or the interwebs, or sitting in front of the television (does anyone have a television anymore)?

5. Daily Practice: Make it so. The visual artist Chuck Close has this great saying: "Inspiration is for amateurs." Indeed.

6. Resistance: Recognize when you're having it. Look it right in the eye. When you find yourself making too many excuses, instead, find a way to get your work done.

7. Unnecessary Drama: The artist's life takes work. Every life takes work. The world we live in is a real trip. So what

can you do? Spare yourself the unnecessary drama. And by "Unnecessary Drama," you know what I'm talking about. Keep the drama on the stage.

PROMPTS

Prompts are very popular. I have two prompts that I give to my students and to myself:

A) Write.

B) Rewrite.

These work well.

WRITING AND REWRITING

In my experience it's been helpful to realize that writing and rewriting are two separate things. Writing: anything goes and everything grows. Rewriting: using your sword of discrimination (your inner editor) and cutting away what's unnecessary. Often we encounter difficulty when we try to write and rewrite at the same time. I write. Then I rewrite.

PERSONALITY MANAGEMENT

Most challenges come down to this: the management of your own personality. Often we spend time trying to control others. Please.

THE SELF

Think big S. The Self is a physical manifestation of the great river that runs through all of us and everything. Little s is your little self, your small-time personal stuff. Yes, your little s stuff needs to be taken care of, so take care of it. And also remember to Live Large. Love Large. Empathy starts in the "heart," informs the whole body, and helps develop the senses.

GENRES

No need to put yourself in a box! Follow the work as it calls you. I write plays, movies, TV shows, lectures, novels, music, songs for my band. I'm not saying be scattershot, but I am saying, if you feel the calling and are willing to put in the hard work, your garden can have a variety of hardy flowers and beautiful vegetables; the redwoods can shoot up alongside the ferns.

PUTTING THE TIME IN

Often when I seem to be having writing difficulty, I ask myself, "Have I been putting the time in?" Difficulty with work is an opportunity to recommit myself to my basic daily practice. And one doesn't need TONS of time. If you have twenty minutes a day, then set your timer and get to work.

THE USE OF THE TIMER

A timer helps focus your energy. I've found this really helpful. I suggest a simple kitchen timer instead of the timer on your phone. For obvious reasons, people. But if it's not obvious: a simple timer allows you to keep both eyes on your work and, yeah, your phone is crack.

LOWERING THE BAR

If you're having difficultly, lower the bar, lower your expectations and then, as the tasks become easier, gently and slowly raise the bar. I do this all the time. Ten pages a day too hard to write? Write five! Write three! Write one! Write one half! It's important to keep showing up. Do what you gotta do to keep showing up.

PARENTING

I have a five-year-old son. I feel that I've become a better writer since becoming a mom. My time-management skills have certainly improved. And so has my guitar playing. And my love life too. Bring it on.

WATCH ME WORK

For the past seven or eight years, I've been teaching a weekly FREE writing/creativity class called "Watch Me Work." It's part performance art, part writing workshop. I've done it all over the country and overseas too. Currently we have class most every Monday, at 5:00 p.m. EST in the lobby of the Public Theater in NYC. If you can't make it in person, we live-stream via Howlround. What we do is work together for twenty minutes, and then I take your questions about your creative process. Come sit and work with us or tweet your questions. So if you *ever* have questions about your writing or your creative process, or if you feel excited and want to share a success or a triumph, or if you feel like you need a second opinion about your work, or if you'd just like to feel less alone while on your creative journey, then come join the class. We're a lively, diverse bunch, all ages and genres and levels of experience, and I'll enjoy speaking with you. For more info, here's the link: http://www.publictheater. org/Programs--Events/Suzan-Lori-ParksWATCH-ME-WORK.

GETTING EASIER

People ask me if the going gets easier when one's been at it longer, when one has achieved things called success and recognition. In my experience the air becomes rarer, the demands greater, the peers fewer and further between (or just so busy that it's harder to connect). There's a lot of positive energy out there. There's also a lot of shit. But we who walk the artist's path, we're among the spiritual warriors. This is not an elevation of your station, just a realization. So, as a spiritual warrior, when you hear your calling, then your burden is light. When you answer and continue to answer your calling, then your burden is light. It becomes light when you say, "Yes, I will do what I've been called to do." Or if you don't know what you've been called to do, then just take a step in the direction that gives you joy. Take some steps, walk the road you're on, pay attention, and—come on—be kind to everyone you meet. It's like climbing Everest over and over or running a succession of ultra marathons. As you walk your path, it gets more difficult, but also, truly, it begets more joy.

SARAH RUHL

I often begin my class at Yale by having the students read Lewis Hyde's *The Gift* over the summer. Hyde talks about gift economies rather than capitalist economies and how art is actually situated in a gift economy. I want to reorient writers away from the idea of having to perform or create a product. When I say performing, I mean not the performing arts, but the obligation to perform like little performing dogs. And I want to move them away from the idea that art is solipsistic, because art is for another person. So the writers read *The Gift*, and then I assign them a recipient writer in the program to write a gift play for. (We also read about small theater, like the happenings in Times Square a couple years ago called Theater for One.) First they interview the person and find out his or her likes and dislikes, and then they write a play for that person. They perform them in this kind of crazy logistical process; I purposefully don't match them up reciprocally, because part of the idea of the gift economy is that you give the gift and that it keeps going—it's not only a back and forth equation. I don't watch the performances, because I think they should be private. That's the ritual we often start the year off with.

Of course I've also stolen many of my assignments from other teachers. Paula Vogel uses the prompt "Write a play that's impossible to stage," which I love, because it's like a zen koan; nothing's really impossible to stage. It's the same with another assignment from Mac Wellman: "Write a boring scene." If you try to write a boring scene, invariably it's not boring. There's one I love from Marie Irene Fornes, which is "Write a letter from your character to yourself." If you're stuck, pretend you're the character and say, "Dear Sarah, you may think you know me, but what you don't know is …" And then you write a whole letter.

117

Some exercises that I've come up with over time: One is to do free writing with the students and tell them to write as if they're translating. They pretend that the scene has already been written in another language by a great master who speaks Spanish or French or whatever language they're interested in, and pretend they are just going in and translating this amazing already written scene. This often frees the writer from the panic about creation and also gives them a little distance from their language of origin.

I sometimes challenge students to write a five-act play in three to five minutes. You have them write at the top, "Act One." You have Characters One and Two (1, 2, 1, 2 down the page) and then in one minute, they fill in the blanks of dialogue. Then you have them flip the page and write "An Hour Later," and the same two people are speaking. Then you write "A Year Later: Act Three," and then you can add a character. And then (you can have four or five acts) for the fourth act you write the heading, "The Moment before the Very First Moment," and make it circular structure. You can create whatever structure or container you like.

In terms of structure, I love to teach Paula Vogel's "Six Plot Forms" because it's good for writers to realize there's not just one form—the Aristotelian arc. There are many ways to describe many structures. Paula breaks it down into circular form, repetitive form, Shakespearean form—which she also calls epic or associative, where the images lead the progression—and then Aristotelian form—which is linear, or based on cause and effect, and looks like an arc. Then she describes something called synthetic fragment—which is two time periods happening simultaneously, like *Angels in America* or *Top Girls*. Then I added one, with Paula's permission, which I call Ovidian form, which is based on transformation, one event unfolding out of another event, a kind of fairy-tale structure where objects have magical properties. Ovidian plays don't necessarily have a moral but take great pleasure in the telling of the tale. Shakespeare's romances rest on this form, and also a lot of visual kinds of playwriting. So sometimes I'll teach these forms to students and then ask them to take a fairy tale and structure it in each of these seven ways.

In terms of dialogue, it's crucial for playwrights to have an ear. It goes back to listening, both as a teacher and as a writer. It's very hard to teach having an ear, if you don't have it, if you don't have a sense of the rhythm of language and the rhythm of living speech, it's almost impossible to teach. Structure I think you can teach, and collaboration, I think you can, to some extent, teach. I think Yale does a beautiful job at throwing writers into the deep end of collaboration, and saying, "Making a play is *making* a play, and you do it with other people. You don't do it by yourself." Playwriting is such a hybrid form, where on the one hand it is literary and solitary, and on another level it's being with people until late in the night making sets and making room for actors to have a living, breathing voice. I think that theater is at its basic root level three things: actor, ether, and language. The playwright is responsible for the language, but if she makes no room for the ether, and if she forgets about the fact that actors are speaking the language, then you have a dead piece of paper.

One exercise I remember Mac Wellman giving, which I think is great for developing an ear for dialogue, is to go around to a café with a little recording device and record real conversation and write it down exactly. Mac's hypothesis, which turns out to be true, is that people talk very strangely. We think people talk in this eloquent way. People talk very strangely, and you look at all the disruptions and leaps in logic in what people are saying when you transcribe it. I think that's a wonderful way to start. Other ways to develop an ear include acting—being inside of plays. Translating a play helps to hear the original. Reading a ton of plays is, frankly, the best way.

Another exercise I love I stole from Shira Piven, daughter of Joyce Piven, who was my teacher—I should mention Joyce because she was my acting teacher (not that I'm an actress, but I did study theater with her and much of what I've learned about how actors used language is from Joyce). So her daughter Shira, who's a film director now, made up this exercise where you divide speech acts up into essays, rants, stories, and poems. You have four possibilities, and someone shouts out a noun, like glasses or spectacles. Then someone else has to say the speech mode (essay or rant). Then you spend two minutes and you write a rant or poem about spectacles. And the more mismatched the better—the more the genre and subject don't match, the better.

What I find liberating about that exercise is that we think a certain way when we think we're writing in a genre dutifully. We think, *Oh, I know what a play is. It has an arc, and characters have objectives*. All these things you might learn in graduate school—I think it really tightens us rather than loosening us. So when you muck around with genre, I think people write more fluidly, and I think plays encompass all genres; they have the poetry of the speech, there's the argument, which is an essay, and then there's the story, the spine of it. I don't necessarily think these little exercises lead to any good writing in and of themselves; I don't think you necessarily would save them and put them in your play. But I like opening playwrights to the idea that they're writers, that they could write in other genres, and other genres are part of their plays. They're not just learning to do this mechanical thing which is called writing a play.

Over the course of the semester, my students bring in pages, and we talk about the pages. And I've been pretty vigilant over the years about using Liz Lerman's wonderful model for feedback (critical response process).

So, basically, the core steps as I teach them are:

1. What you love. The audience says what they found meaningful, evocative, striking, and exciting in the work.
2. Artist as questioner. The artists asks their burning questions about their own work.
3. Then the audience can ask questions as long as the questions do not have an opinion embedded in them. This sometimes takes time to teach and model – the question that does not mask an opinion.
4. Comments and opinions. The audience offers opinions subject to permission from the artist. The form in which the opinion is given is set and is "I have an opinion about X. Would you like to hear it?" The artist has the option to say no.

I instituted the Lerman model in my teaching after I experienced it at New Dramatists. I had always thought it was a bit prescriptive and not organic, but then when I experienced it first hand as a writer, I thought, *Oh, we must do this.* Because actually, you're often not ready for criticism until you've had some nice things said about your work. Because truthfully, when a writer brings in raw, vulnerable pages, all they want someone to say is, "Oh, I loved it." That's really all you want to hear unless you have a degree of self-loathing, and once you hear some nice things you're ready for criticism, like taking a warm bath before scrubbing off dead skin.

I remember when I first started teaching at Yale, there was panic in my students' eyes when they were about to get feedback, and I thought, *Why do they look so panicked? Like sad little deer!* I knew Paula Vogel had created a culture that was very generous, and I knew the writers to be generous to one another. I thought, Why the panic? When I did Liz Lerman's method, I discovered it formalizes the progression of when you hear what. So you know whether you're about to get something nice or not nice, and it really diminishes panic. Because if you're braced for it—if someone says, "I have a suggestion. Would you like to hear it?" You can say, "Okay. I'd like to hear it." Or, "No thanks, not right now." Whereas if you're looking around the room not knowing if someone's going to say, "Oh, I loved it. That changed my life," or "I really couldn't find my way into that," or even "your play made me really angry," every time someone makes a comment, you feel slightly panicked. So I love that Lerman formalizes a critical progression.

I also created a course at Yale called "actor workshop," which was funnily enough based on my own search for preschools for my children and reading about Maria Montessori, who had the concept of the teacher-less classroom, where the children would go into the room and discover knowledge on their own. They would have something called "the manipulatives," which were little tools. I thought, *So in graduate school, what is the teacherless classroom? What would it look like?* and I thought, *Oh, actors are the manipulatables!* Because actually, as a playwright, you can learn almost everything you need to know from listening to actors do your work. There's only so far you can get hearing a teacher lecture you about dramatic structure. What you really need is for a good actor to come in so you hear if your work is off, or you hear when your work is really working. You can hear when it's really alive, and you can hear when it's dead. I have the writers run the room with the actors and hear what they need to hear, and they can choose not to have feedback. Usually they choose to hear feedback from actors, but they can also choose to say, "I just want to hear my play."

Over the course of a few years with my students, I love having more discursive time, more one-on-one time, because sometimes I feel in a workshop setting it can become too much about product and getting through the pages and critiquing product rather than talking about the art form over the long haul. Process can be more intimate, and involves more than writing. So in their second years, the students come to New York, and we go to places like New Dramatists or Sam French so they can walk through the door of those places and feel confident about their ability to be there. I call that class "Places of refuge for the playwright." Then we can go deeply and individually into their work in a place that makes theater all the time. And I tailor the reading list to the individual playwright based on what he or she is working on. I do love organizing a class around a reading list, but generally when I'm workshopping plays, I don't like the writers to feel constrained by a giant reading list that the whole class shares. I like to tell them what I think they should be reading based on what they're working on. Then, at the end, they write a manifesto that can be very personal.

I also teach a class called "Ovid and His Influence," where we read *Metamorphoses*, and then we read all these playwrights who I think are influenced by Ovid, like Chuck Mee, Maria Irene Fornes, Elizabeth Egloff, Mary Zimmerman, Julia Cho, Jorge Cortiñas, August Wilson, and Adrienne Kennedy. And we write plays that have traansformations at the heart of their structure. The plays have to have one song, one magical object, one sudden transformation, and one non-human.

So the above are little tools, little tricks, little exercises. But at the end of the day, teaching is a relationship. And teaching can be a relationship that's marked by power. To not notice that, I think, can be very, very dangerous, especially when you're dealing with art, because it's so vulnerable. You need to have a sense of respect and boundaries around the material that students bring to you with their whole heart Teachers should not try to carve out little homunculi—little cutout versions of themselves. It's good for teachers to know their own aesthetic well enough to know when they're trying to stamp it on their students, and this is so hard to learn. No one wants little acolytes, no one wants twenty million Mac Wellmans running around, like Mac Wellman 2.0. Nobody wants that. Least of all Mac!

The best thing a teacher can do is help students strengthen their own voices rather than misdirect them into another voice or vocal pattern that's actually the teacher's. Sharpening one's listening is really important. Empathy is really important. Doing no harm in the Hippocratic model is really, really important.

I think it's wonderful if playwrights can go to graduate school. The reason I say this is not a platonic belief in the goodness of playwriting programs but instead a recognition that at this historical moment, this is how playwriting communities are formed. In the Renaissance you had the Medicis; now you have MFA programs. It's our system of patronage and our system of finding a community. Maybe in the seventies it was easier to find your community just by picking up and moving to New York—now, less so. Many of these programs are funded. It's helpful to have time and money to write a small body of work when you're starting out instead of working five jobs and not having time to write.

The situation of graduate school is an artificial system—constantly having feedback and criticism. And it's great practice for the world where playwrights increasingly have that same situation. I want my students to learn to be like whales; whales have these enormous sieves where they can just take big gulps of water and automatically differentiate the krill from the stuff they shouldn't be eating. I think graduate school is a place to practice being a whale and developing your own sieve before you go out into the world and have to figure out which notes to keep and which to discard. I want to teach my students how to feel empowered enough to go out into the world and say, "Thank you very much for that comment. I'm going to think about that." Sometimes I've even chanted that phrase with them: "Thank you very much for your comment," as opposed to thinking, *Oh God, I have to immediately go home and fix my play*. There are so many people in the business of fixing plays in the contemporary world of theater—I think that's changing a little bit—but playwrights need to learn how to go into that situation with both confidence and humility.

I think there are also risks of studying playwriting in a formal setting if you're in an environment that shuts you down instead of leaving you open. Martha Graham has this wonderful quote: "It is your business to keep it yours clearly and directly, to keep the channel open. You do not even have to believe in yourself or your work. You have to keep yourself open and aware to the urges that motivate you. Keep the channel open…. No artist is pleased. [There is] no satisfaction whatever at any time. There is only a queer divine dissatisfaction, a blessed unrest that keeps us marching and makes us more alive than the others."

There are some programs where people feel shut down and closed down rather than opened up, which produces a lot of self-loathing. And for students who are in that situation, the risk is that they stop writing. I would say to those students, "Find a way to protect yourself for the next two years, or go to a different program." I advise them to keep the channel open, so that whatever our contribution is, we can get it out into the world before we die.

I'm inspired by my students and their writing and by their passion and their optimism and their hunger. Recently when I was at Actors Theatre of Louisville working on a new play, two of my students' plays were there too. Brendan Pelsue had a play called *Wellesley Girl*. And Hansol Jung had a play called *Cardboard Piano.* They wrote both plays in my workshop and I adore them both. So I took them out to dinner to celebrate in Louisville, and I bought a nice bottle of wine. I felt very celebratory, and it made me feel very grown up and very happy. I was literally sharing the stage with Brendan; our plays were on the same set. It made me gloriously happy to share the stage with them. Teaching is cyclical and generative; there is the moment where you say to your student, "You're my colleague now." This cycle goes back to the gift economy and the idea of giving and knowing that the gift will keep going.

I'm so grateful to my teachers, like the great Paula Vogel. I don't think we honor the teachers of playwriting enough, because we're obsessed with originality in our culture, so we don't want to admit that we've been taught. I really believe in the concept of lineage, and the concept that in any of the arts you have teachers teach you form, and you're responsible for content. Someone still teaches you how to sharpen your pencil, whether it's your mother, or your art teacher who teaches you that you have to sharpen your pencil with a knife. We shouldn't be ashamed of that knowledge being passed on. We should be proud of it.

Octavio Solis

Most of my students are new to writing. The primary thing that I work on is getting them to simply write without judgment and reasoning—to write from a very different place than they think they are supposed to write. Many of these writers have been trained to write essays, theme papers, documents that engage the more analytic part of the brain. I want to access the angelic brain. I want them to approach their writing not through the front door but through the most unexpected windows.

On the first day I offer exercises that will cause them to pass the pencil over the paper with as little conscious thinking as possible. In the beinning, I don't mind if they choose a different form. The initial writing can take the form of a poem, a first-person account (diary), a short story, or a monologue. It doesn't necessarily have to be theatrical. I encourage that. Eventually I'll guide them toward more dialogue and less prose, but first I just want them to feel comfortable with the idea of writing something on paper that is meaningful to them. I want them to get to a place where they can access a strong image with as little anxiety as possible, and from there the words usually find them.

I use a variety of exercises, but all of them involve visualization. I acquired this idea from my workshop working with master playwright Maria Irene Fornes. In her lab at INTAR Theatre, she took us through many daily exercises that were instrumental in breaking down my presuppositions about what makes a good play, making me available to a very different kind of head space in which real creative writing could truly happen. As an acolyte, I credit Ms. Fornes for most of the work I do in the classroom, even as I have altered many of her exercises to suit my teaching style.

All exercises in my class begin with relaxation. One can't write when one is tense. If the writers are relaxed, so relaxed that they're almost sleeping, they'll be in a better state of receptivity. This is vital for my process to work.

I start by asking them to close their eyes and, in their mind's eye, go to a place that is special to them. Without dictating what it should be or what it should look like, I guide them along the way by asking for details in the appearance of this place; everyone sees something different. I always remind them: don't make it up. If you don't see anything, wait. Wait until it comes. If nothing comes, that's all right; be patient. Generally, something always comes. They reach into some deep well of their being, and from their past, something is offered to the writer. Usually something unexpected. That's the thing about receptivity: one just has to be ready, available and present for the moment. I ask them what they see. Of course they're not talking back to me, they're only listening. But I ask them if there are people there, and if there are, what they are doing. Then I ask them to listen, just listen, and again, remind them not to make it up; don't invent dialogue.

Sometimes for the sake of entering into the kind of spell that I require for these exercises, I start with some kind of countdown—but a dynamic countdown. I ask people to see in their heads a hallway. I instruct them to walk down the hallway. There's a door. Open the door. I never know whether there's a staircase that goes up or down, but either way it goes up to an attic or down to a basement. Every house in our dreams, even if it's the one-story house we were raised in, has an attic and a basement. It's where we keep our memories. It's where we keep the relics of our unconscious past. I always take ten steps to go up there, and I have them count each step. I take a long time to get to the top or bottom. Everyone taking the exercise has to see the steps that they take and not get ahead of me.

Either that or I have them actually visualize the number ten, with their eyes closed, in a specific font, a specific color, and have them stare at it for a while before asking them to erase it and then see the number nine. I take them slowly in this countdown back to the number zero and ask them to let the zero grow larger and larger. Then I ask them to step through the hole of the zero.

When they come out the other side, I ask them where they are.

It's a different place. Look around you. Discover where you are. Look to the left and then slowly to the right and remember what you see. Then pan again, and realize that you missed this person standing there. What does this person look like? How is this person dressed, how is he or she standing, or what is this person doing? Is this person sitting at a loom? Sitting on a bench crying? Writing a letter? How old is this person? What is the attitude? What is the look in this person's eyes? I ask them questions while they observe the scenarios unfolding before them.

After all that, I say, let a name come to you. If it doesn't come, just call him A or her B. Eventually, a name will come. Maybe not until somebody calls out the name. Then I ask them to let this person speak aloud. Who is this person talking to? To us? To someone who is present but unseen? To herself? What does this person want? What can you intuit from this person? Sometimes it's not even about seeing actual people in a room. Sometimes it's pictures on a wall. There's someone in a frame on a wall. Who is that? Perhaps the people are in a photo album. See the people at different times in their lives, at specific important occasions. By asking questions, I take the writer through a specific trek across a vivid landscape and time that is entirely new and fresh to them.

Once they begin to see a place and people populating it, I offer some suggestions. I don't plan them ahead of time, and it terrifies me a little because I never know what I'm going to say when I'm in the room during the exercise. Sometimes I don't even know how I'm going to start.

I'll have them close their eyes and then I'll hold my breath and wait for something to come to me. I've done these so often now that I have a repertoire of suggestions that I can use in a pinch, but I never rely on them. I count on finding the right image to help the writers find their way in. I need to be available for them in this exercise in the same way I am asking them to be available. I don't pre-plan, and it can be harrowing sometimes, and my stomach can be in knots because I just don't know if I'll have something to say to keep them "in the zone," so to speak. But something always comes. I simply have to be available for the vibe in the room to tell me where I should begin. We chat when class starts, and somebody might mention something about a dog that got hit by a car, or about something that was on the news last night, or about a break-up in a relationship.

Some of those things may strike my antenna, and recalling them I'll say: "There's a dog." Or I might say, "There's a letter opener. There's a letter opener on a desk." Or someone reaches into his pocket and discovers a letter that wasn't there before. What is the letter? Who is it addressed to? Open it. Read it. What does it say? It can be anything. I can suggest a change in the quality of the light. What is it? Did the bulb burn out? Did someone turn off the light? Did someone open a window? Is the sun finally setting? Something changes in the room in terms of the light. What is that? Or perhaps there's music coming from somewhere. Singing. What is the song about? Is it a recording? Is it live? Who's singing? And why?

So just as I take them in with a countdown, it's with a count-down back up to ten that I bring them back up. I always feel like this process is a bit like open-heart surgery, and if I'm going to do that, I'd better make sure to close them up. Close up the sutures and return the same way. I liken it also to deep sea diving. Come up slowly and carefully, or you'll get the bends.

Once they are back, I ask them to take the blank paper in front of them and write what they saw and heard—what they remember. I never tell them, "Write a scene." That's why sometimes the form takes a non-dramatic structure.

At times, they write down exactly the journey that they took down there. "I went down there, and I saw this and they were saying this, and then I thought it was this." And that's all right too. There's no wrong way to do the exercise. There's no failure. The only failure is consciously making up details that are meant to be dramatic, that are meant to impress me or the class. We can always tell when that happens, when they're trying too hard to be good writers. So every-one writes from this space, a special, private place about things they didn't think were important—things in their past, sometimes things that were in the past three, four, five generations before, or two weeks before. Sometimes they have no idea what it means; that's actually a very good place for them to begin. I always tell them that they've created a place of mystery. You've created something that intrigues you. And if it intrigues you, we'll be intrigued as well. We want to know what will happen next.

It's at this point that they are finally writing in the exercise, and it's a single, sustained, uninterrupted session, sometimes for forty, forty-five minutes. In the very early stages, it's usually a brief thirty minutes, but after that I increase the session length. I don't tell them how much time they must write—I'll only say to start writing. I give them a countdown so they know how much time they have left. But at some point I'll say, "Ten minutes," and they have ten minutes to work and finish the scene, and then "five minutes," and then "one minute" to finish up. I tell them at the end to take some notes so they can pick up the thread again later. But I ask them not to feel compelled to finish the scene during the session. Just come to a stopping point.

During the writing sessions, I direct them to keep their pens moving forward, the hand moving forward as they write. Even if nothing is coming, even if they've come to an impasse, I ask them to keep their hands moving over the page even if they are doing squiggles, even if they are writing the same word over and over and over again until they find their way back in. I make sure they don't turn back to read their earlier pages. To keep them from freezing up, I advise them to just close their eyes and go back to that space—that room—where they saw what they saw and listen harder and wait for another cue, another signal, for something else that will get them going again. Because what usually happens during these stalled moments is they start to make it up— they stop trusting and start to concoct things, which makes the writing feel ham-fisted and forced; it no longer feels organic, no longer seems to come out of the experience that the characters are having because there is a need to finish the scene.

Sometimes they finish the scene way too early. There will be half an hour left to go in the writing session and they are done. Or, rather, they think they are done. I'll tell them to keep writing. Even if it's done, keep writing, keep talking. Even if one of the characters left, have them come back in and keep talking, and they will find that the scene wasn't done. They just quit because it was convenient for them to close it. They went with a nice little bow on this scene for the closing, rather than follow through with what was going on—which requires a breakthrough to the kind of text that they do not expect.

During the writing, I have all these quiet prompts that I give them. I might say there's a pair of scissors—someone uses a pair of scissors—and I tell them to write that in their margins and use it any way they wish. Some will do that, but I'll also tell them to ignore it if it doesn't help. Sometimes they use it to force the scene to break out of its circular rut, which is perfectly correct. But usually (remarkably), the prompt lands in their writing right when it is needed.

I give them these prompts to shake up their train of thought. They may be following a really great thread and think, *Oh I know where this is going. I'll take it that way.* So I'll throw in an unexpected prompt, like someone coming in with a bouquet of flowers, and, suddenly, the writers have to deal with that. How do they incorporate that? Can they incorporate that? It derails their train of thought, causing them to invest instead on a more interesting way to go from point A to point B—not the direct route that they customarily see. Maybe in the end their play will go that route, but incorporating something nuanced and wondrous will make it more interesting.

As writers, we always start with chaos and work toward order. We want meaning, but sometimes we don't give ourselves the benefit of the doubt that the meaning will reveal itself in its own time. We needn't dredge it up right away. Everything shouldn't be explained right away. It's perfectly fine to live in the mystery and to leave open some dark spaces. Otherwise we start moving into the realm of the well-made play.

As they write, sometimes for an hour straight, I always tell them, "Don't stop to read what you've written. Keep your hands moving forward. Keep the eye moving forward. Follow the thread." I tell them the muse will not wait for them. I say, "In the time you're reading, you're dropping out. You don't want to drop out. Stay with it."

I also tell them that going back and reading means you're being an editor. I don't want you to be an editor at this point. When you go back and start looking at your writing, you start judging it. You start thinking, *Ow, this is a terrible line. Oh, this is awful writing*, and you start crossing out lines. I don't want to hear any cross-outs or erasures at all. Or you look at it and think, *Wow, this is impressive. This is really good.* But then everything has to be that good.

I don't want them to be good. In fact, I tell them, "Don't try to be excellent. Don't give me your best writing. Don't give me good writing. Just write. Just write. Don't try to be excellent. That's part of the later process called craft. That's editing. That's when you bring your editor in. But you don't want your editor in the room when you're creating new writing. In fact, your editor shouldn't be in the room until you've built a significant body of work. You don't know what the story is. You don't know what you're cutting. There might be a line that seems to stick out and feel incongruous or nettlesome, and you might want to cut it. Then later you discover that it was the most important line in the whole play. If you're honest in your writing, you don't know what's important until you've got it all down. Once you've got the whole play down, then go back and cut. In the meantime, just kept moving forward."

The third part of the phase in these exercises, after visualization and writing, is reading. We always read the work that is created in the room, and I allow time for us to share it. It's very important. It's part of the fellowship, part of the safety net for people to be able to share work. As the writer reads aloud what he or she wrote, I ask the students to write down things that they remember from what they hear: special phrases, things they found fascinating, moments they were mystified by. But never any notes of critique. These sessions are not about critiquing and saying, "Well, I think you could have done this better. I thought this character was weak, blah-blah-blah." We don't critique because the writing that happened in the room came from a special place, from deeply vulnerable spaces, and must be respected. Moreover, they've had no time to do any revisions, no time to think about it and apply craft to the work. They're just writing and sharing something that's deeply raw and personal. How can you critique that? So I don't permit it.

The act of reading aloud enables them to hear what I consider their true voice. That's vital. They get to hear a voice they didn't know they had. And everyone else listening gets to hear this special voice too. Speaking the words aloud has the effect of putting the tempo and tone of the work in one's own mouth, and therefore a new and immediate sensory experience instructs the writer on what he or she has written. It also makes the other writers thrilled when the writing takes on this special voice. *How can I go there?* they wonder. The only way to go there is not to listen to someone else's voice and imitate it but to find their own voice in the writing. All students work according to their own internal engines. They shouldn't compare their work to each other in terms of number of pages or the amount of material that is produced. Some students will produce up to ten pages in a single sitting. Others will only do two and some will only do one and that's okay. Everyone develops according to his or her needs.

Nor does everyone come in at the same level. I get students who haven't written a play before, yet they are allowed to take the time they need to find their rhythm in the work. There always will be someone who shines and seems really good, but everyone has something to say. I believe every person has at least one important story to tell—a good writer knows how to spin that tale into many different stories. But everybody has one good story inside, and if they don't tell it, we'll never know it. And no one else will be able to tell that story the way that they do. So I try to impress upon them that they should trust their voice to find that one story that must be told their way, and that it is vitally important that it be put it out into the world. If they don't tell it, it disappears—it dies with them. This is something I stress in the room.

Thus we start with any kind of writing and then move toward playwriting. Usually, by the second class, I introduce a second character into the visualization, which initiates dialogue. As soon as you have another voice in the room, you have a play. Then, in the course of the third or fourth exercise, I introduce a third character, but by that time many have already done it themselves. They're already kind of finding a way in. So we'll do a series of these for quite a while.

Something that happens when they are working together in the room that I find remarkable is how they communicate through the zeitgeist with each other, while they are writing. They are so quiet and intent on their own work, but something is happening in the room, some communal thing. When we then read our own work, we are often amazed at the interesting connections that arise between two or three writers in the room. Sometimes all of them. They will, by happenstance, bring up a specific object or a specific theme or a specific name, which I haven't introduced. That's very exciting because it indicates that they are being responsive to each other without realizing it. It's in the air; their antennae are picking up cues and using them, which means they are collaborating with each other in a tacit way. That's miraculous when it happens.

As they're writing, they discover what the story is. I tell them, don't force it. Let the characters guide the story for you. Of course, the writers are already gently guiding it. It's always them, but I offer the illusion that they're actually giving up the reins of control to the characters by telling them to let the characters tell the story. They know it—they know the story better than you do. If your characters are full and free and have agency, they will know where to take the story. Listen to them. Wait and follow their lead.

It takes a tremendous amount of trust not only in the process but in one's own voice, one's own artistry. But eventually they come to understand what the shape of this new beast is, this play. So after we have done a few exercises, we work from what they've written. The scenes they have been writing might be from different worlds—different characters from different stories that have nothing to do with each other, all composed day to day, I ask them pick out what they think they would like to pursue. Which has a thread that they feel compelled to pick up and continue? Which of these works is going to possess them?

An exercise I sometimes do with my students involves the introduction of craft. We take a scene and start by underscoring with a highlighter the most important lines and significant moments in the work, or even write them on separate page. Then I ask students to start telling the next scene. What's the next scene between these characters? What's the next moment? Then I ask them to write the next scene, and I do a visualization that enables them to write it. And they write, just write, and once they're at the finish line, they go back and cut. Then they can look at the work and say, "Well, this isn't part of this play. This is a part of a different beast. This is another play." They excise these. Make this thing more elegant. Learning elegance is part of craft—trusting one detail to tell the truth and not just continuously trying to express everything.

In the novel *Nutshell*, I read the line, "Don't unpack your heart." You need to be simple. You need to be a little more elegant, to find out what the pointed thing is that can cut through everything. What can you not say? Find the simple gesture; create more air in the room.

Every play is different. There is no formula. I don't give them exercises on play structure because everyone will find their own frame. I might mention a play that some should read that will bring up a similar structure to what I see working in their particular work. But it's hard to generalize about form when these students are already very different—when they're writing plays in such varied, highly original forms that require their own attention. So it makes a lot of work for me.

I tell them not to worry about things that seem impossible to stage. I tell them that's a director's problem. The director and the designers will solve this. If you write in a waterfall, trust that a director will put a waterfall on stage and make everyone believe it, most likely without even using a drop of water. I tell them not to censor themselves when they think, *Oh, that can't be done in the theater.* The theater is a place of magic, and the audience helps create that magic. We've all signed a virtual contract that says we're going to believe together. Trust that your collaborators will help make the world you imagine come to life.

My teaching is more about being available to the magic of the work and less about craft. It's about how to generate a lot of material in a defined period of time. But I do provide the opportunity to think about craft. It's all subtle and it's in little bits and spurts here and there. I'm not very good at lecturing, so I don't lecture students about craft much at all because the writing they do in the room is about exploding all these ideas, all these formulas, and reconfiguring them according to the work. I can only discuss it in terms of context, in terms of what's happening in the room with this writing right now. I tell them, "Listen to this in your writing. Become aware of this. See what they just did? This is really beautiful—it's so beautiful, what he's done here or what she's done here. Do you know how this happened? This is something a director can sink her teeth into."

I do it in that context. The more formal bullet points of playwriting become relevant only when they turn up in the work. Otherwise, when I start talking about these things, they start changing the form of their work to suit the structure, and that's wrong. They need to honor the organic frame of this beast. This new animal, they have to discover how it breathes. It's comes out whole cloth, and they have to figure out how it lives. They have to figure out the physics of the world in which the beast moves. Every play has its own rules.

It is important to keep the writer in the same state of surprise and delight that the audience feels when they see a play. Too many times, we as writers already know what the story is, what's going to happen in it, and how it's going to end. Everything is all laid out, and we just need to write it and the character fulfill those roles—they fulfill their function rather than the other way around, which is to find the characters and then find out where the story goes. It could even be the same story but it will be more organic if it comes from them. So it is important that the writers find the zone where they listen more than they are accustomed to. I think it's the kind of process that poets undergo. They just need to follow the thread. They can always go back and fix what's wrong. Clean it up later. In the meantime, get it all out—be ugly, be messy, be perfectly flawed.

By the end of the term, I always feel like we didn't get enough done, like we didn't get to the end. And that's because the writing in the class has to progress toward some kind of reading or performance. So everyone shifts from still creating and making discoveries to "let's present this now." And that process is rash and hurried and sort of goes against my own better instincts. My writers are still discovering what their plays are, and there is pressure to present them before the are complete. We're already putting up skyscrapers and inviting people in to come see them. I am not comfortable with that. I'm in the process for the long haul, and I want them to be in the process for the long haul too. It feels like the class should just end and resume again the following term. So I feel inadequate in the process. At the same time, that's often how work in the theater goes. You start writing, and then all of a sudden you have an audience in two weeks! You scramble to finish scenes and you're rehearsing and then boom: you have a show. And I'm not interested in the show as much as I'm interested in exploring who these people are. The work of the play still calls for more exploration. I guess that's what it is about. I'm more interested in the exploration than the product. But the product is what we're finally looking to complete.

At the end, I always mention the *Dramatists Sourcebook*. Everyone needs to find this book and subscribe to it every year. You can find it online. The *Dramatists Sourcebook* gives you places to submit your work. But I tell my students, don't just rely on that. Find your company. Find your people. They're out there, those who will trust your voice, your particular vision. You're not writing the well-made play, so chances are you're probably not going fall in with your local community theater. But there are some companies out there that are looking for your specific kind of work—adventurous, innovative, mysterious, haunting. There are companies that will want to take that ride. You need to get to know them, engage with them, and then collaborate with them. Hopefully they will trust your vision and there won't be any conflict, but be prepared! Because sometimes the first thing they want to do is change your play. So as a playwright, you need to trust your own voice in the process. The craft of playwriting is so different from any other kind of form of writing because half of it is solitary and the other half, by necessity, is extremely social and collaborative. The work becomes a blueprint for everyone else's work. So much depends on the writer's availability to that process. But it's very hard to trust your voice and find that now you have to listen to them, to allow their creativity. A play must be permeable enough to absorb everyone's creative input and still maintain its shape.

I tell them to find that company, find that family that responds to you and your work. If you can't find it, build it. Build that family yourself. That's how I started out. I submitted my work and nobody was interested, so I said, "Hell, I'll do it myself. I know actors, know about directing. I've got a stage here at this funky new wave club I'm bartending at. I'll do it myself here. I'll pay people out of my own pocket. Twenty dollars." You'd be surprised what people will do for twenty dollars. Just do it, and then watch. If the work is good, if the work is honest, watch them come to you.

I want them to care about their work so that it becomes something really important to them. I think the best stories a writer can tell are ones that are already inside them, rolled up in the flutes of their bones. They are there. The stories are all there. You don't have to go to some topical thing. Because fascinating as they might be in the moment, these topical works will surely be revised and worked on perhaps for years, so writers better care deeply for them, because if they don't, a director will. A designer, a producer, an actor will care more for the work than the writer will, and that's not a condition a writer ever wants to be in.

But if writers are writing from a place where the stories are so deeply embedded in them, they will care about these stories more than anyone, always, because they're part of them, an extra appendage. Then the writers are going to invest in the work long after it's finished. As long as they write from that special place, they will know how potent and dangerous writing can be—how eternally powerful.

The Best Advice from Master Playwrights:

Working on Craft; Starting Your Play; Revising a Draft; Community, Sustenance, and Perseverance

The chapters you have read contain extraordinary advice and encouragement for developing writers. These master teachers speak about perseverance, sustenance, and preparation of the artist. They also provide concrete and valuable advice and methods with which you can approach the various steps of writing a play. Here is a review of a few great tips you'll want to remember.

Working on Craft

As you prepare to write your play, how do you engage with the many elements at your disposal, advancing dialogue, characterization, and structure? As experienced writers and teachers, many of our authors have exercises you can try when you're interested in working on particular elements of craft. Carlos Murillo offers this exercise as a way to explore character development:

> I ask students to come up with a list of ten to fifteen alternative names for themselves. The guiding principle for choosing the names is the following: imagine the different personas you inhabit in different circumstances and moments in your life— for example, who is the you on a first date? Who is the you when you are on a vacation with your family? Who is the you when you are jealous or angry

139

or in love? Is there an aspect of your personality that is still an adolescent? Is there a crotchety eighty-five-year-old curmudgeon lurking inside you? Is there more than one gender, sexual orientation, or ethnicity cohabiting within the multiple personas that comprise your character? Do magical beings or superheroes or supernatural or superstar figures coexist with the ordinary and mundane? I encourage my students to think beyond the pedestrian and expand their imaginative limits when conceiving these alternate names. The second step of the exercise: find visual images corresponding to each persona. If each of these people existed in the world as autonomous beings, what would they look like? What sort of clothes do they wear, how do their bodies inhabit space? This dossier of images form the basis of a sequence of writing exercises aimed at generating characters, worlds, and the seeds of a play.

Murillo also encourages a deeper understanding of character with an exercise that asks students to engage in physical and sensory details:

I ask the students to choose a name/image from their dossier—preferably a persona that feels very distant from them that day. I have them spend time studying the image closely, making note of every apparent and implied detail they can extract from it. I then talk the students through a sensory exploration in which they imagine what transformations their own bodies would have to undergo in order to inhabit the body of their persona/image. From there they explore physicality and movement: How does this person move through space, what do their legs, arms, spines, feet, faces feel like? Taken together, how do these physical sensations shape the sounds made by the voice?

Follow the process through for two or three characters and then begin writing a scene.

Borrowing an exercise from Holly Brown, Quiara Hudes re-iterates Murillo's use of self in developing character, asking writers to list all of their identities. She encourages them not to only list those that are obvious and safe, but to include those they might not wish to share. She encourages continued work until you "really get to a level of complexity and honesty and enigmatic nature of all the opposing identities someone can have within."

Once you have the list, put them together in triangles of traits that do not necessarily align. Quoting Paula Vogel, Hudes calls these "character recipes." Envision a character with the three traits in the triangle and write a monologue, for it is often oppositional qualities that make complex characters. Hudes notes, "Outside obstacles are important for characters too, but alone they do not provide sufficient depth to a play."

This foundational work is important and enables you to avoid what Steven Dietz describes as trying to make a play "interesting—to make the characters busy doing really interesting things." He warns against too many "bells and whistles" at the expense of truly examining character. He encourages "looking for literal moments when a scene comes to life," moments he calls Turns: an escalation, major new information, a reversal, a surprise, a paradigm shift—"all things that when we're watching a scene keep pulling us in." For practice, he recommends writing a short, two-to-three-character scene in which there are three turns on every page; "So there's a surprise or a reversal, and those can be enormous or those can be tiny."

Part and parcel of characterization is dialogue, and Ruhl describes an exercise she borrows from Mac Wellman that is useful in developing your ear: "Go around to a café with a little recording device and record real conversation and write it down exactly. Mac's hypothesis, which turns out to be true, is that people talk very strangely ... I think that's a wonderful way to start."

Hudes also has writers flex their dialogue muscles by challenging them to think more creatively with the text, to "surprise her a little more with your words." She suggests working with twenty lines of "straightforward dialogue": "You're fired." "Wanna make out?" "I know you're cheating on me." Then rewrite these lines in a new and original way, distinct to a few different characters. Write a series of straightforward responses to the first set of lines. Then rewrite these responses in the voices of new characters. Hudes finds that "this is a way to wrap our minds around the fact that sometimes the most direct way to say a line isn't necessarily the most musical or creative or fun or artistic."

Sarah Ruhl recommends freeing yourself from preconceived notions of language conventions with a translation exercise:

> [I] tell them to write as if they're translating. They pretend that the scene has already been written in another language by a great master who speaks Spanish or French or whatever language they're interested in, and pretend they are just going in and translating this amazing already written scene. And what this does is to free the writer from the panic about creation, and also gives them a little distance from the language.

With character and dialogue underway, Ruhl also has an exercise that pushes her students to play with the structural construction of their work:

> I sometimes challenge students to write a five-act play in three minutes. You write at the top, "Act One." You have Characters One and Two (1, 2, 1, 2 down the page) and then in one minute, they fill in the blanks of dialogue. Then you have them flip the page and write "An Hour Later," and the same two people are speaking. Then you write "A Year Later: Act Three," and then you can add a character. And then (you can have four or five acts) for the fourth act you could say, "The Moment before the Very First Moment," and make it circular structure. You can create whatever structure or container you like.

Quiara Alegria Hudes uses recognizable stories to encourage a deeper understanding of structure in her students. Working with a plot from an established story (she uses both Humpty Dumpty and the life of Jesus), students write monologues for one moment in the story.

> Then we read those monologues chronologically. Then we'll switch up the order, follow some other plot forms. We'll read them reverse chronologically.... Then we'll read them out loud as a circle play, so chronologically then going back to the first one. We'll use the same writing in different ways, and it's a great, clear, very fun way to talk about how structure can shed a whole different light on the same exact story, on the same exact words,

and how much freedom there is in structure and how essential that is to the storytelling.

Lucas Hnath encourages writers to consider style or voice by having you write as if you are a playwright whose work you have read. Start with a monologue. "Now write it as Anne Carson would write it. Write in her voice. Then write it in the voice of Fornes. Then write it in the voice of Churchill. Then lastly I say, now write it in your own voice." Hnath notes that the act of writing in a style of another writer is extremely useful in starting to recognize one's own voice.

Hnath also describes an exercise in exploring the relationship between problem and action that is helpful in developing storytelling skills in motivation and plot movement. He suggests reading a play and then dissecting and listing all the problems the characters have in the play.

> That quickly fills one column. Then you can have a second column next to that and have a little arrow drawn off from each problem, "and so what?" The character encounters this problem, and so they do what? Then you list the actions the character takes in the play as a result of each problem. The movement between problem and action is really easy to find in a very wide range of different plays from different traditions. It's really easy to break down a play into a chain of problems and actions. And then I find that once they see this in a play that they didn't write, students have an easier time seeing the possible relationship between problem and action in their own play.

Even as you're advancing specific mechanisms of your craft, these teachers encourage you to continually question, to think outside the box, to see what you don't immediately see. An exercise Ruhl borrowed from friend and director Shira Piven is useful in freeing students from the self-imposed confines of traditional genre conventions.

> You divide speech acts up into essays, rants, stories and poems. So you have these four possibilities, and someone shouts out a noun, like glasses or spectacles. Then someone else has to say the

speech mode—(essay or rant). Then you spend two minutes, and you write a rant about spectacles or a poem about spectacles. And the more mismatched the better—the more that the genre and the subject don't match, the better. What I find liberating about it is that we think a certain way when we think we're writing in a genre dutifully.

Kron has also developed an exercise that encourages a way of recognizing the difference between thinking within our preconceived notions of objects or events and approaching them with openness and honesty. She recommends writing a "version of a story [you've] told but to use the present progressive voice"—in other words, to write it moving forward in time rather than looking back. So for instance, rather than saying, "Then I went down the stairs and there was my dog, looking pleased as punch …," they'd quickly move to unfolding action: "I'm walking down the stairs. Oh, there's my boy, there's my Rover. Rover, no! Put down Sissy's hamster!" In so doing, writers can free themselves from their own instinctual need to predetermine the action of a play, which can deny the potential for discover.

But it's not only the dialogue and structure that might need examination, and Hudes has an exercise that forces a reconsideration of use of stage directions—a key and sometimes overlooked aspect of playwriting. By challenging writers to write directions that cannot be literally staged (an impossible sword fight, a hurricane), she encourages in writers the development of the skill of suggestion. But in opposition, she also reminds writers that the most exiting moments of writing need not necessarily be extreme. She also asks writers to "write a stage direction where there's no artifice, zero illusion:"

What's happening in the story is literally what's happening on stage. Someone drinks a glass of water. Someone sweeps a floor. These sorts of literal moments ground us anew in the material world that we live in. The make believe, the pretend, must yield to the magic of reality and of bodies on a stage. One of my favorite ones is: "A tailor enters, sits at a sewing machine, and begins to sew a dress." By the end of the play the dress is complete and the lead actor puts it on. The magic of reality.

Regardless of the writing task, Lisa Kron advocates a five- or six-minute reflective writing about the experience. She says she learned from Madeleine George that "asking students to do a short writing after an exercise or a discussion about what came up for them that surprised them or interested them is an extremely useful teaching tool. It gives students space and time to make their own connections between whatever they've just done and their personal writing goals."

Beginning a new play can be intimidating, even daunting. Beth Henley acknowledges that the task of beginning can be terrifying, recognizing how "difficult it is *to begin*, because it's just a white piece of paper." Thus, our playwrights have offered, throughout the book, an array of approaches that may be helpful as you embark on a new project.

Steven Dietz has valuable advice for the act of beginning a play, dispelling a common block to writing; i.e., waiting for "an idea." Dietz says, "The idea for a play can be generated. The idea does not just have to be "found."

He advises not to wait for a "complete idea," noting you can always find an image and proceed from there. So start with the image:

> You're going put that in action, and then you're going put that action in time. A necklace? Great. So if your image was that necklace, I'm going to encourage you to put that image in action. Suddenly, you'll have a character in your play. And that character's taking this necklace off and putting it in a small box. What is she doing? Why is that girl putting that necklace in that box? So you put the image in action: a young girl is putting the necklace back into a box.
>
> There's still nothing there, story-wise. *The moment it comes alive is when you place it in time. When* is this girl? *When* is this moment in her life? Not what era. When in her life? Her mother has passed away. Simple. Yes. Immediately I have a character. I have an event. I have a moment of *kairos*, a threshold moment for her. And now whatever the girl does with that necklace will give me something:

if she refuses to wear it, if she sells it, if she saves
it, if she remakes it. And story will follow, no matter
which route I take. Image in action, action in time.

Octavio Solis also believes that a writer does not have to wait
for external inspiration. He believes the story you need to tell is
already contained within you, and he uses an approach called visualization to enable writers to discover new settings, characters,
and scenes. He guides his students through this practice, but you
can do it alone.

> I start by asking them to close their eyes and in their
> mind's eye, go to a place that is special to them.
> Without dictating to them what it should be, nor
> what it should look like, I guide them along the way
> by asking for details in the appearance of this place;
> everyone sees something different. I always remind
> them: don't make it up. If you don't see anything,
> wait. Wait until it comes. If nothing comes, that's
> alright; be patient. Generally, something always
> comes. That's the thing about receptivity: one
> just has to be ready, available, and present for the
> moment.... I never tell them, "Write a scene."

Such guided visualizations enable writers to find inspiration
within their own creative imaginations. What they discover is the
place from which writing begins.

Lucas Hnath often writes using specific individuals or events
from history as a starting place, so he guides his students through
that approach:

> I do an exercise that involves going and reading the
> newspaper and finding a story that feels like it has
> a play in it and bringing that back and then we play
> with it. Or since I've written a number of plays about
> celebrities and historical figures, I might ask them to
> use a famous person as a starting place. I'll have
> them write out things they know about this famous
> person—a hundred things I know about the famous
> person. Then I have them put a star by the problem
> that they find most interesting, and then I have them
> write about an event in their own life where they had
> a problem that was similar. I ask them to recount the
> memory, then write the memory as a scene.

And as you begin, Beth Henley reminds writers to leave the critic at the door: "It's not your job to think if it's good or bad. Just keep the channel open. That will let you off the hook. You are not going to be Shakespeare. You are going to be you."

Finally, these teachers encourage you to find and protect time and place for writing. Henley encourages writers to: find a space where they will not be interrupted; turn off all electronics; and do this for a clearly timed four hours. (Doing it in two sessions is allowed.)

Perhaps the best advice is to just get to it—write without hindrance—write without excuse.

As Suzan-Lori Parks notes: "I have two prompts that I give to my students and to myself:

A) Write

B) Rewrite.

These work well.

REVISING A DRAFT

Congratulations, you have a draft of your play! Now what? Your work has only just begun. Our playwrights offer many ideas for how you can approach revision, but ultimately, most of them encourage objectively critiquing your work while staying close to the joy of the process.

To begin, Suzan-Lori Parks offers a distinction: "In my experience, it's been helpful to realize that writing and rewriting are two separate things. Writing: anything goes and everything grows. Rewriting: using your 'sword of discrimination' (your inner editor) and cutting away what's unnecessary. Often we encounter difficulty when we try to write and re-write at the same time. I write. Then I rewrite."

Quiara Hudes speaks to just reading your work out loud as a valuable way to note places of challenge within the work:

> It's helpful for a few reasons. A skill that's useful as a playwright is selling your own writing. Commit to the line. Say it out loud with clarity. Another is that when you've written a full length play, and you have to sit there and read all of those characters out loud, you can actually—now this is a muscle that one hones with practice—but you actually will start to notice, "that page was really fun to read," or "that page gave me the chills," or "my mind has been

wandering for the last page and a half." It's those reactions that I want the students to take note of. Most especially, when does it feel most alive? Those five pages that feel most alive, you want your whole play to feel that way. When do you check out? When do you get bored? When are you going fishing, in your mind? Notice those pages. That happened for a reason too.

Octavio Solis echoes Hudes and develops his students' ears for voice by having them listen to their own work:

The act of reading aloud enables them to hear what I consider their true voice. That's vital. They get to hear a voice they didn't know they had. And everyone else listening gets to hear this special voice, too. Speaking the words aloud has the effect of putting the tempo and tone of the work in one's own mouth, and therefore a new and immediate sensory experience instructs the writer on what he or she has written.

Steven Dietz asks playwrights to "look at their own work rigorously," to learn to "walk around their ideas, their plays, and apply strategies from differing angles." He says playwrights must "learn to invite (rather than wait for) scrutiny." He also describes how he ruthlessly rids his own drafts of "traps":

The traps I point to are answered questions, stated emotions, transitional phrases, double sentences. Now, of course, there can be answered questions and stated emotions and transitional phrases and double sentences in your play—but eventually these things, alone or in tandem, will spell the end of any motion in your scene.

For "rigorous" examination of drafts, Dietz has his students track the major questions on each page:

It's a great exercise to write at the top of every page what the question on that single page is. And I don't mean theme. There's no help for you when you descend into theme. When you descend into theme you can say, "Well the question is really about can love conquer the trappings of a difficult family?" That's fantastic. I can't direct that. I can't act that.

You can't revise that because there is nothing tangibly there. What's the real and present question on the page? (And don't sweat if it's simple.) When will Brenda arrive? Great question. Doesn't have to be artful. Turn the page, page two, what's the question? When will Brenda arrive? When will Brenda arrive? If I have the same question at the top of the page for, I don't know, fifteen to twenty pages, what's wrong? Perhaps everything is wrong! Unless the energy system of the play is built around the arrival of Brenda, the play is not moving. And even if it is, we are hungry for other more present and proximate questions as we wait.... If I have the same question at the top of page after page after page, I know there hasn't been a shift. There hasn't been a turn. There has been no narrative motion.

When sending students back in to look critically at their writing, Kron encourages examination of the play's action. She encourages her students to tell her "what is transformed from the top of the play to the end. If they're rewriting I might ask them to see what happens if they put, say, three transformations into the scene they're writing."

Murillo recommends thinking visually as a way of approaching structure in order to examine potential holes or bumps in the progress of a play: "What is the first image? What might be a possible last image implied by that first one? Can you imagine a sequence of key images that will take us from beginning to end?" Murillo proposes a practical, visual, tactile solution—visual mapping—that helps you see a play with a new clarity: Write the main actions of each scene on individual cards and post them up on a wall. The visual before you will reveal the action of the play and any barriers to its forward motion.

Hnath recommends seeking a bird's-eye view of your work, a process of distilling out essential elements. He encourages writers to read a great play and then condense the play down to thirty lines of dialogue and twelve stage directions. The objective is to reduce the writing in such a way that you can read through those lines and those stage directions and actually get the story. Then he encourages writers to do this with their own plays—at two different times in the writing process. Early on he encourages writers to "just race ahead. Try to write out the whole play in thirty lines." This results in an outline in the character's voices that can provide key guidance as the writer progresses. Then he suggests reducing one's play in order to become "conscious of the play's most essential elements."

If you're jammed or struggling with a particular moment/scene/character, Jon Robin Baitz suggests stepping outside traditional playwriting and examining your play from a new perspective:

> I ask a student who is stuck in a particularly gnarled knotted ball of a problem to rewrite the scene in the form of a letter from each character to the other, thereby taking it out of the world of necessary dialogue and into a more psychological one where you are weirdly empowered by description. Then you can take those two letters and retranslate them in some way, with as few words as possible, into the scene you are having trouble with.

Baitz also notes that writers must keep exploring their own work, mining it for new discoveries and unlocking new doors:

> Everybody needs to remember that the only thing that makes sense is a mysterious process where doors are locked and there is an infinite number of doors until there are very few doors left. But they might not see the last few doors in this house, in this room, in this tunnel. If you keep asking questions, if they are the right types of questions, this unlocks the door. Sometimes this is accelerated. If you write a play very quickly, this is accelerated. But sometimes you may reverse engineer the play. The doors are still there.

COMMUNITY, SUSTENANCE, AND PERSEVERANCE

Suzan-Lori Parks writes, "While we often work alone, it's helpful to realize that we're in this together." Jon Robin Baitz says quite simply, "Collaboration is essential," and his colleagues agree that community is vital for writers. It's for this reason that Sarah Ruhl advocates for a formal school environment: "Playwrights should pursue formal study, and I advocate for graduate school. The reason I say this is not a platonic belief in the goodness of playwriting programs, but instead a recognition that at this historical moment this is how playwriting communities are formed." Baitz knows that writers "can learn by being around younger writers or newer writers for a concerted period of time where you are just you—if you are a practitioner of the theater."

Beyond school, always seek community. Octavio Solis recommends to each writer, "Find your company. Find your people. They're out there, those that will trust your voice, your particular vision."

Deitz says:

> If you want to continue to hone your craft as a playwright, you also have to find your mentors and find your group—finding that group of playwrights to hear your plays.... Rub yourself against the playwrights who don't write the plays like you do. Self-produce on a small scale. Don't write your masterpiece. Write the play in front of you. Make a great collaborator, which is different than finding a great collaborator, make someone your collaborator.

Ruhl continues with Solis's exact words: "Find your people. Find a community of writers who you can create deadlines with and share work with, because it's really not a solitary activity. That's one thing that differentiates it from writing poetry or novels; in order for it to be finished, it needs to be read out loud by a group of people. So find that group."

These masters also recognize the value of true collaboration with the other theater artists who bring a play to life. Dietz says, "Find a director or a dramaturg you love. Put them in your pocket, and then make sure you work with a wild card person every now and then." Solis advises, "trust that your collaborators will help make the world you imagine come to life." Baitz also advocates for the insight of experienced director:

> I also think playwrights need great directors who really hear them in ways they can't hear themselves....Sometimes you even need other people to read it, because you are too close to it. It always helps to have someone very, very smart, usually a director that you have a relationship with—an experienced director who can help you.

No matter how much training, input, or advice a writer seeks and absorbs, Dietz reminds us all, "We want writing made simple. It's not. It never will be."

So what does a playwright do when the going gets tough? Parks writes of her own work, "Often when I seem to be having writing difficulty I ask myself, 'Have I been putting the time in?' Difficulty with work is an opportunity to recommit myself to my basic daily practice."

Indeed, all of these veteran playwrights emphasize the need for daily practice. They advocate for discipline that includes writing every day—regardless of whether a writer feels that there is specific work to be done.

Henley advises:

> It's important for my students to understand that the
> act of writing itself has value. It doesn't matter what
> you write, just that you write. Discoveries will be
> made, ideas will come. There will be times when
> you are not inspired to write. The theory of writer's
> block is just part of the process.

Advice from Parks: "Daily practice: Make it so." She quotes visual artist Chuck Close: "Inspiration is for amateurs." Parks continues, "Resistance: recognize when you're having it. Look it right in the eye. When you find yourself making too many excuses, instead find a way to get your work done. Unnecessary Drama: the artist's life takes work … keep the drama on the stage."

These teachers emphasize the need to persevere, even when the play in front of you has become less compelling or difficult to pursue. Hnath describes it as a much-needed drive playwrights must possess: "There comes a moment in every playwriting process where the honeymoon ends … [but] sit with it and move through it and find that drive to fight through the relationship that's gone sour but still has potential, the fight to pass through the honeymoon phase."

Once the excitement of starting the play and even, perhaps, getting the first draft done, has passed, the work must be pursued. Murillo notes, "It's challenging because the novelty … has worn off, leaving [writers] vulnerable to self-doubt and second guessing. Many of the students will have the impulse to jump ship and start on something new. I have a hard and fast rule that they must follow through with what they started, and learn to love the difficult process of shaping their play from these raw materials."

Keep at it, advises Dietz:

> Write the play in front of you. Keep doing it. It
> sounds so simple. Do that daily work. Whatever

your daily practice is. Make sure you have a daily practice. We must talk about what we control and what we don't. We don't control the new play market. We don't control a thousand things, but the one thing we do have control over is that we have twenty-six letters and thousands of days. We can do our work. There's nothing between us and the art form. There's all sort of things between us and a career. There's nothing between us and the art form.... So what do we control? We control rigor.

While it may seem obvious, Murillo reminds writers that they have to love what they're doing: "In the end, I teach process and loving all the effort, trial, error, discovery, and euphoria that comes when you start with nothing, a blank page, maybe some ideas in your head and journey toward a complete thing. I believe that is a hugely valuable life lesson."

Perhaps the most potent counsel comes from Sarah Ruhl, who says, "My best advice to young writers is go for it. We're in a renaissance of playwriting."

Heed Octavio Solis: "Keep your hands moving forward."

About the Editors

Dr. Joan Herrington is Chair of the Department of Theatre at Western Michigan University and a contemporary theatre scholar whose research is focused on the pedagogy and practice of theatre in the last twenty-five years. She is the author of four books that examine the creative process of playwrights and directors. She has also written more than a dozen book chapters and journal articles appearing in Journal of *Dramatic Theory and Criticism, American Drama,* and *The Drama Review,* and she served as editor of the prestigious publication *Theatre Topics.* Through her research and practice, she has explored modern theatre around the world and engaged theatre artists from Japan to Great Britain to Nigeria.

Dr. Herrington has taught workshops at many universities, and her work as a director and dramaturg has taken her from coast to coast with productions in New York and Los Angeles and as far as the Edinburgh Festival in Scotland.

Dr. Crystal Brian has been a Professor of Theater at Whittier College in California and at Quinnipiac University in Connecticut for twenty-three years. She has written journal articles and chapters in a number of books. These include work about drama therapy with veterans, drama therapy with inmates, and improvisational theater in Nicaragua as a part of the Albert Schweitzer Institute. She has written extensively about Horton Foote and is currently finishing a book about the playwright. Dr. Brian is also a director and playwright whose work has been seen in Los Angeles, New York, and New Haven. She is currently writing a play about veterans, war, and PTSD that will be performed at the next Nobel Laureate Summit in 2018.